Blair A. Ruble

The Arts of War

Ukrainian Artists Confront Russia
Year Three

Blair A. Ruble

THE ARTS OF WAR

Ukrainian Artists Confront Russia

Year Three

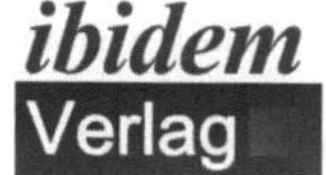

Bibliografische Information der Deutschen Nationalbibliothek
Die Deutsche Nationalbibliothek verzeichnet diese Publikation in der Deutschen Nationalbibliografie; detaillierte bibliografische Daten sind im Internet über http://dnb.d-nb.de abrufbar.

Bibliographic information published by the Deutsche Nationalbibliothek
The Deutsche Nationalbibliothek lists this publication in the Deutsche Nationalbibliografie; detailed bibliographic data are available on the Internet at http://dnb.d-nb.de.

Cover: Photo of a man in military uniform at the exhibition of Nikita Kadan in Drohobych (Ukraine) in summer 2022.

ISBN (Print): 978-3-8382-2070-3
ISBN (E-Book [PDF]): 978-3-8382-8070-7

Leuschnerstraße 40
30457 Hannover
Germany / Deutschland
info@ibidem.eu

Printed in the EU

Table of Contents

1: Introduction

All these essays except for chapters 48 and 49 appeared in the *Ukraine Focus* blog of the Kennan Institute at the Wilson Center over the course of the third year of the Russian invasion of Ukraine. Those last two articles were scheduled to appear when the blog came to an end.

The series grew from my need to respond to the horrendous events unfolding before me. Previous work relating the arts to social and political developments in Ukraine and Russia led me to turn to the work of Ukraine's artistic creators to better understand what has happened, is happening, and will happen.

I, like many, have been moved by the steadfastness of Ukrainians in the defense of their country. The stories presented here highlight the ways in which they have long explored the meaning of their country and culture through the arts, and the way the arts and their creators have empowered Ukrainians to confront the Russian invaders. They offer intriguing clues about the culture, society, and politics of a postwar Ukraine.

These essays also represent my attempt to provide Ukrainian artists a place where they can speak for themselves. I have been fortunate in being able to collaborate in the preparation of these articles with many of the artists mentioned here. Aside from the introductory and concluding essays, I have striven to keep my own voice in the background. I follow a variety of performance and visual art endeavors across the country to capture the expanse of Ukrainian creativity. The 50 pieces here follow the third year of profound resistance to the February 24, 2022, invasion, and a striking creative resilience. Like those in my essay volumes on the war's first and second years,* these tales reveal a deep reinvention of various art forms as a distinctive Ukrainian artistic voice consolidates.

All the essays in this collection were written during the war's third year, even though several were posted following the conflict's

* Blair A. Ruble, *The Arts of War: Ukrainian Artists Confront Russia, Year One;* and *Year Two* (Stuttgart: Ibidem Verlag, 2023; 2024).

third anniversary. With one exception, they were posted in the order in which they appear. The exception is the article written for the war's anniversary, which is placed last.

The essays may be read chronologically, or by artistic genre—music, dance, theater, video, the visual arts, etc. Readers may turn first to those set in specific locations: Kyiv, Kharkiv, Lviv, Odesa, and so on. Alternatively, readers may direct their attention to the multiple connections, financial and creative, that have emerged between Ukrainian artists and the international community. Or they might search out the many moments when Ukrainian civilian and military authorities have endorsed the performing arts as a means of advancing their country's fortunes. However these essays are approached, I am confident that even the most informed readers will discover a depth and creativity to the Ukrainian artistic scene that they hardly suspected existed prior to the Russian invasion.

2: New Lights in the Shadow of War

April 5, 2024

As the war in Ukraine continued at a barbarous level last March, the Lviv National Opera's ballet company premiered an ambitious new work, *Light from the Shadows,* grounded in the third part of Mykhailo Kotsyubynsky's important novel, *Shadows of Forgotten Ancestors.* Based on an original libretto by Vasyl Vovkun and music by Ivan Nebesnyy, this innovative ballet, featuring more than a dozen dancers, could well become a staple of postwar ballet repertoire.

Kotsyubynsky's novel of star-crossed young lovers has inspired many artists to bring its tale of young love, clan conflict, witchcraft, and folklore to life since its publication in 1912. Ivan and Marichka, a couple from two rival Hutsul families in the Carpathians, seem ready-made for stage and screen. The first ballet based on the novel, with music by Vitalyn Kyreiko, premiered in 1960. Sergei Parajanov's internationally celebrated film of the same title followed in 1964, set to an acclaimed screen score by Myroslav Skoryk. An adaptation to mark Kotsyubynsky's centennial was performed in 2014.

Kotsyubynsky wrote his lyrical and philosophical novel following a visit to the Carpathian village of Kryvorivnya in 1910. The settlement is just north of today's Ukrainian border with Romania in the western Ivano-Frankivsk region. The Hutsul inhabiting the area remained pagans until well into the 20th century and celebrated a magical world hidden in the surrounding mountains. Their tales and lifestyle fascinated Kotsyubynsky.

The Hutsuls, whose language is a dialect of Western Ukrainian, most likely originated as a mix of Slavic tribes who fled to the Carpathian Mountains to escape invading Mongols during the 13th century. Once in the mountains, the Hutsuls developed their own distinctive folkways.

The origin of their tribal name is lost in time, perhaps having been derived from the Romanian word for *outlaw,* or the Slavic word for *nomad.* Known for colorful craftsmanship in clothing, woodworking, and pottery—as well as for their traditional songs and dances—the Hutsuls became a prime subject for folkloric studies as 19th- and 20th-century transportation and communications systems encroached on their isolation.

Kotsyubynsky, a provincial (*zemstvo*) statistician fascinated by local folkways, was known for his picturesque portrayals of traditional customs and peoples. He authored several collections of ethnographic tales as well as nearly two dozen novels (including the sprawling *Fata Morgana,* published in parts between 1906 and 1910). His interest in local traditions brought him into recurring conflict with Tsarist officials until his death in 1913, at the age of 48.

Today's two-hour retelling of Kostyubynsky's tale of romance, sorcery, and death marks an eminent achievement for the artists involved, especially given the war that raged while they worked. Librettist Vovkun enjoyed a successful theater career in Lviv and Kyiv before serving as minister of culture and tourism in the second government of Prime Minister Yulia Tymoshenko between 2007 and 2010. Composer Nebesnyy studied with Skoryk, the composer of the celebrated score for Parajanov's film, before continuing his training in composition in Austria. He is the founder of the contemporary music ensemble Cluster, which has performed widely over the past 30 years around Ukraine, Europe, North America, and Asia, and he directed the Kyiv Music Fest between 2006 and 2012. Lithuanian artist Arvydas Buynauskas, who created the sets and costumes, is a rising star in European theater design.

The Lviv National Opera has been among the first Ukrainian cultural institutions seeking to return to a modicum of normality following the Russian full-scale invasion in February 2022. The company presented a full schedule of well-known works this season, including the operas *Carmen* and *Don Juan* and the ballets *Don Quixote* and *Esmerelda.* Housed in one of Ukraine's most storied theaters, and away from the front lines of the war, the company has tried to provide a respite to audiences that include soldiers, evacuees, and local residents.

In a turn to the future, the company has also drawn on support from Western partners to mount new works such as *Light from the Shadows*. By doing so, it offers a hint of a postwar Ukrainian culture that looks forward as well as back.

3: You Can Take the Boy from Kyiv, but You Can't Take Kyiv from the Boy

April 12, 2024

Like many international icons, choreographer Alexei Ratmansky transcends national labels. Having grown up in Kyiv, he trained in Moscow before returning to his hometown to dance. Later he became a star lead with the Royal Winnipeg Ballet before dancing and later choreographing for seemingly every major ballet company in the world. He spent time as director of Moscow's Bolshoi Ballet, and had returned there to choreograph a new work when Russia launched its full-scale invasion in February 2022. He left the country the next day.

The current war cemented Ratmansky's identity as Ukrainian. As he has noted, not only did he spend much of his childhood in the Ukrainian capital, but his parents still live there. Marina Harss's recent biography of the choreographic megastar, *The Boy from Kyiv,* makes his connection to the place clear. Despite President Putin's proclamation that there is no such thing as Ukraine, the people he studied and worked with over many years in Moscow had no doubt. Ratmansky remained an outsider within the cloistered world of Russian ballet. He was, and forever will be, "the boy from Kyiv."

Ratmansky seemed to be running too fast to worry about any label prior to 2022. He had projects everywhere, much to the dismay of some balletomanes who didn't always appreciate his style. After 2022, Ratmansky left no doubt that he is Ukrainian. He proudly stood center stage waving a Ukrainian flag during curtain calls for the provisional United Ukrainian Ballet's world tour of *Giselle*.

Ratmansky marked one of the most important evenings of his career in February. For his debut as artist in residence at the prestigious New York City Ballet (one of the top five companies in the world), he created an emotionally wrenching ballet about the current war, *Solitude*. As *New York Times* reviewer Gia Kourlas wrote,

> "dancers waver and buckle as inner and outer forces wreak havoc on their bodies. Within this stark, dark universe, set to music by Gustav Mahler, bodies live on the edge, leaning and bending precariously as they fight for equilibrium. They are disjointed, their body parts at odds with one another. Spines twist deeply, as if wringing out the torso could also unleash the rawest pain."

At the center kneels a solitary man—Gordon—wearing an army-green President Zelensky-styled turtleneck. He is motionlessly holding the hand of his dead son. Dancers spiral across the stage, with pairs reaching out to others but never finding solace. Gordon suddenly springs into the air with a solo of swift jumps, drifting across the stage as if a ghost. His grief is overwhelming.

Ratmansky based his ballet on a photograph of the body of a 13-year-old boy killed at a bus stop in Kharkiv, his father holding his hand for hours. The ballet master brings the father's lament—and the horror of war—chillingly to stage.

At the close of her biography of the choreographer, Harss observes that "something in him has cracked open" with the war. Ratmansky was no longer the superstar of the international ballet world; he now felt connected to place (specifically New York and Kyiv). He has become fully Ukrainian. "Meanwhile," Harss continues, "this new sense of love and allegiance and responsibility toward Ukraine has led Ratmansky back to a place that, in a way, he is only now discovering." As Harss recounts, Ratmansky told an interviewer in mid-2022 that "'My identity is really broken,' so 'I will need to find a way to glue it all together.'"

Ratmansky's need to put various parts of his identity back together is shared by thousands of his compatriots who now find a world in which their Ukrainianness matters more than they ever imagined it would. Like so many émigré artists before, Ratmansky gives voice to the constant uncertainty of expatriation. His work makes clear that Ukraine exists within displaced Ukrainians, waiting to be bonded back together once this catastrophic war ends.

4: How Do you Feel Fear? Young Ukrainians Answer on the New York Stage

April 19, 2024

For the past two years, more than a dozen Ukrainian teenagers from cities as diverse as Kyiv, Lviv, Ternopil, Kosiv, and Kharkiv have been writing short plays about their wartime experiences. Their works depict a new everyday norm, as many are scattered to countries like the United States, Spain, Germany, Austria, Romania, and Poland. Others have remained in Ukraine. Drawing on a shared sense of survival humor mixed with absurdity, the young playwrights have captured the sadness and painful uncertainty of living during a war. Their works will be coming to New York in May.

The plays emerged from an ongoing collaboration that grew from New York-based screenwriter Laura Cahill's video course during the coronavirus epidemic. Cahill, whose long list of writing credits includes work for both stage and screen, was teaching private workshops when COVID-19 hit in 2020. She moved her courses to a virtual platform and continued teaching and mentoring her students online. She received an offer to repeat her course for a group of teenagers who would log on from their homes in Ukraine after she had wrapped up her first pandemic-era classes. Her work with these students began in October 2021 and was to have ended on February 6, 2022, as Russian troops began to mass along Ukraine's borders.

Having developed a relationship with her Ukrainian students, Cahill reached out to see how they were responding to the increasing Russian threat. Once the invasion took place—just 18 days later—the students scattered. Some remained home, others found sanctuary elsewhere in Ukraine and in Europe, and others moved between home and safe places, in the constant motion that characterizes many Ukrainian lives over the past two years.

Cahill urged the young writers to reflect on their personal experiences in new scripts, which she made available to the entire group for discussion. She mobilized her network of professional actors to perform an online reading of her students' first collection of short plays, *How Do You Feel Fear?* in July 2022.

Lars Rudolfsson, director of the Orion Theatre, Sweden's largest avant-garde theater, saw that reading on Zoom and asked if he could direct the works in Stockholm. The Orion put on the plays 30 times throughout the spring as graduation performances for young Swedish actors, accompanied by Ukrainian cellist Anna Nuzha.

Back in New York, Cahill enlisted a distinguished group of mentors and guest artists who continued to work with the Ukrainian playwrights. The result was the Young Playwrights Ukraine Ten-Minute Play Project, performed on Zoom in August 2023. Two collections of the group's plays will be published by theater publisher Smith & Kraus.

New York's Vineyard Theatre has agreed to host the North American premier of several of these 10-minute plays on May 6. A renowned off-Broadway theater just off Union Square, the Vineyard is a natural home for this performance. The theater has been hosting "multi-art chamber theatre" for more than four decades, according to its website, earning a reputation as an incubator for "collaborations across art forms." The Ukrainian works reflect the venue's core values of "integrity, creative risk-taking, and nurturing a diverse community."

The authors of the Young Playwrights Ukraine project offer the promise of a vibrant Ukrainian theater once the war has come to an end. Their works hint at new writing and productions beyond what had represented Ukrainian theater prior to the war. Their collaboration points to a vibrant scene that will command attention from theater professionals in Europe, North America, and beyond. The New York performances next month provide the opportunity to glimpse that future now.

5: Learning from Emigrants Past

April 26, 2024

The 2022 Russian full-scale invasion of Ukraine touched off a creative firestorm in Ukraine's theater community. Playwrights set out to capture the terrors of confronting war; actors, directors, producers, and established companies collaborated to keep theater companies together as circumstances allowed. Those in theater mobilized to demonstrate the mistakenness of Russian claims that there is no Ukrainian culture.

New plays giving expression to the horrors of war sprang forth. Scores of original works appeared in translation at readings around the world. New Ukrainian works appeared in London, New York, Buenos Aires, and Hong Kong. After some initial minimalist readings, several new works moved into full production.

In Ukraine, theaters reopened their doors as soon as martial law restrictions allowed. Initially, shows tended towards escapist works intended to strengthen morale. Over time, plays explored questions about Ukraine's new realities. What does it mean to live in a city under attack? Be a refugee? Be a soldier for the first time?

As war, tragically, became normal, some theater companies—often with international funding—began to look back, as well as forward, to discern new lessons in works that were thought to belong to the past. A recent production of Polish playwright Slawomir Mrożek's 1974 play *The Emigrants* at Kyiv's Theater on Podil reveals how applicable its insights are to the lives of Ukrainians in the 2020s.

The experiences portrayed on stage mirrored Mrożek's own exile. The play shows an odd couple, a displaced intellectual and a relocated manual worker, trapped in a dank basement as an old year turns into a new one. They initially dwell on their differences in economic status and background. Over time—through raucous wit and satire—the two discover that their experiences are more alike than not. Both understand the privations of being poor immigrants as they acknowledge that both know what canned dog food tastes like, and neither can figure out when the new year arrives, as neither has a wristwatch. The play's absurdity and familiarity made it a cult classic in the Soviet Union of the Brezhnev era.

Mrożek's life reflects the upheavals of the Cold War. A young hack writer when coming of age in Stalinist Poland, he later questioned his youthful enthusiasm for the Communist regime. In 1963, he and his wife traveled to Italy, where they defected, and the playwright emerged as a major critic of the Polish regime. Five years later, he moved to France, where he would become a citizen. He returned to Poland in 1996 but left again, to live in Nice a dozen years later. He died in France in 2013.

In his lifetime, Mrożek continued to travel and to write, proclaiming the absurdity of totalitarian regimes through his plays. In 1975, famed director Andrej Wajda produced *The Emigrants* at Kraków's venerable Stary Teatr. This and other Mrożek works would come to symbolize the demands of the Solidarity movement in the 1980s.

The new staging at the Theater on Podil resonates with the past as well. Noteworthy Ukrainian director Vitaliy Malakhov established Kyiv's Theater on Podil in 1987 in response to the first wave of political and cultural opening under Mikhail Gorbachev's perestroika policies. The theater has come to rank among the city's most prestigious. Its prominent location in the historic Podil neighborhood and its 2018 reconstruction, which earned the European Mies van der Rohe Award in 2019, has added to its luster. Malakhov remained director until his death in 2021 due to complications from COVID. In 2022, the theater appointed distinguished actor, and former member of the Ukrainian Parliament, Bohdan Beniuk as temporary artistic director for the period of martial law.

The current production of Elena Kataeva's new Ukrainian translation of *The Emigrants* has played in repertoire since October 2022. Performed by veteran—and beloved—actors Sergey Boiko and Mykhailo Krishtal, this production appears on the theater's smaller Igor Slavinsky Stage, which is well suited to the constraints imposed by martial law restrictions on public gatherings. *The Emi-*

grants has become a story of contemporary Ukraine. Tens of thousands of Ukrainians now live in emigration, facing the trials, heartbreaks, and absurdities that Mrożek's Poles once did.

6: Revitalizing the City through Sticky Culture at a Time of War

May 3, 2024

Lviv gained an impressive contemporary art hub last December, despite the ongoing war with Russia. After nearly a decade of planning and construction, the Jam Factory Art Center opened at a former food processing plant in a run-down industrial neighborhood about a mile and a half from the city's Opera House. It immediately became the city's largest cultural and artistic center.

The brainchild of Swiss historian and philanthropist Harald Binder, the center has been designed both as a showcase for contemporary art and as a focal point for community cultural life. Comprised of exhibition halls, lecture rooms, a musical space, and public areas open to those living nearby, the Jam Factory is intended to act as a catalyst for neighborhood economic revitalization.

Housed on a neo-Gothic industrial campus dating back as far as 1826—although most buildings were built in the late 19th century—the stunning rehabilitation serves as a catalyst for community activities. As Executive Director Bozhena Pelenska explained at the opening, "In the conditions of war, we have completed a comprehensive revitalization, expanded the team, and prepared an important exhibition and a broad public program. Despite the war and numerous obstacles, we are reaching this long-awaited moment and collectively writing a new chapter in Ukrainian art history."

The center's initial exhibition, "Our Years, Our Words, Our Losses, Our Searches, Our Us," presents works by Ukrainian artists over a century and a half, explicitly highlighting connections between past and present. More than 70 artists—including Alevtina Kakhidze, John Object, Zhanna Kadyrova, Oleksiy Sai, Piotr Armianovski, Nikitia Kadan, Sasha Maslov, and Vlada Ralko—provided images exploring how the war, beginning in 2014, has reshaped society and relationships in profound ways.

Among these works are Elena Subach's "Tuesday, 2023," recording the wrapping and storage of public art around the city for safekeeping during Russian air attacks; Yaroslav Futymskyi's photographic triptych catching images of random passersby the morning of Russia's February 24, 2022, full-scale invasion; and Anton Saenjo's powerful photographs of the everyday wartime routines of his fellow citizens. These images find melancholy resonance with Taras Shevchenkoi's drawings "Fire in the Steppe" from 1848–1849. In addition, Crimean native Yuri Yefanov's "Cube" offers a video of a concrete box standing on the coast near the Artek children's camp as a reminder of what he lost with the Russian annexation of Crimea a decade ago.

Volunteers from the Livyy Bereh (Left Bank) initiative provided the exhibition's largest work: "Theater of Hopes and Expectations." They reconstructed the home of a Kyiv family which was destroyed by a Russian rocket during the invasion's early weeks. The wood came from a city park in Germany and symbolizes society's postwar rebirth.

The Jam Factory represents the arrival in Ukraine of dreams and ideas derived from European experiences linking urban revitalization and artistic invention. Cultural entrepreneur Binder has long been active in Lviv, with this project representing an extension of his previous initiatives. In 2004, for example, he led the establishment of the renowned Center for Urban History of East Central Europe. Housed in a renovated Art Nouveau period town house designed by Ukrainian architect Ivan Levynskyi, the center has become a respected partner in international research projects, conferences, and publishing ventures.

Like the Center for Urban History, the Jam Factory combines Binder's interests in built and cultural urban ecosystems. As Binder told *ArtDependence Magazine* in late December, "We don't want to be perceived as a museum or an exhibition hall. We want to be space for meeting, learning, discussing, and sharing experiences."

Imagined before this war, delayed by both the coronavirus pandemic and the invasion, the Jam Factory has shaped its mission in response to the ongoing upheavals faced by Lvivians and Ukrainians. Binder's and Pelenska's vision of mobilizing culture to revitalize urban life confirms community spirit at a time when resilience rarely has been so important.

7: Don't Forget and Don't Forgive

May 10, 2024

The Russian full-scale invasion of Ukraine in 2022 prompted Ukrainian rapper Skofka (Volodymyr Samolyuk) to write songs giving voice to his generation's anger and sorrow. His profanity-infused wartime song "Don't Forget and Don't Forgive" ("Ne zabudem i ne probachim") excoriates those who speak of building bridges while burning them down instead. The song's last lines—"Guess that's how it feels when you fear everything / I guess I'm done"—captured the sense of betrayal felt by many Ukrainians of his generation when the Russians launched their invasion.

Later in 2022, Skofka released "Hear the Anthem" ("Chuty himn"), dedicated to his friend Valentyn Konovodov, who died in the fighting. The singer's anger had turned into resolve by the time he composed this second tune, and his voice extended beyond any one generation to reach all Ukrainians. Charting the destruction inflicted on towns and cities across the country in a determined and unblemished voice, Skofka returns to the powerful refrain, "In a clear sky thunder's heard / In the sky's a whistle, but the hymn is heard! / In a clear sky there is dense smoke / Mountains sputter, but the hymn is heard!"

"Hear the Anthem" has become an anthem itself for wartime Ukraine, viewed on YouTube more than 10 million times. The piece has been used at times of personal reflection and of communal gathering. It has been sung by soldiers at the front, and by those at home who have lost too much to recover their former lives. It has become the background to film and television reporting on the war and has empowered thousands of individual Ukrainians to find inner strength they did not know they had.

The now 30-year-old Ukrainian rapper was enjoying a rising career with nearly a half million followers on Spotify when the war started. He began recording in 2017 and kept gathering fans throughout Ukraine. In 2021, he joined with Kalysh band leader Oleh Psiuk to record "Dodomu." Several collaborations followed, which were hits on Shazam, Spotify, and iTunes. By year's end, he had signed on with the ENKO label.

Like many of his generation, Skofka had turned to rap to tell his own story and those of his friends. Born in the western provincial city Rivne, he initially pursued rap as a hobby (much to the chagrin of his police officer father). He trundled off to college, after graduating from Zdolbuniv School No. 6, to study business and marketing at a local branch of the Kyiv Slavonic University. Commodity research and the ins and outs of commerce, however, failed to hold his attention. He preferred, instead, to experiment with new sounds and images which told stories of social consequence. Forays into the world of rap prepared him for powerfully articulating the hopes, fears, anger, and sorrow of his compatriots once the war began.

He's travelled abroad to share these feelings recently, with a 15-city North American tour. In February and March, he raised tens of thousands of dollars for the Ukrainian defense effort with shows in Seattle, Cleveland, San Francisco, Los Angeles, Chicago, Miami, Philadelphia, New York, Toronto, Vancouver, and a handful of other cities.

American audiences turned out in the hundreds at venues that wished to demonstrate continued support for Ukraine. His concerts included both fans connected with Ukraine and those who simply love rap. For those already familiar with his songs, the tour provided a welcome opportunity to hear Skofka in person. Others were taken with his poetry and with songs unrelated to the war. Whether knowing Ukrainian or not, fans resonated with the emotions unleashed by "Don't Forget and Don't Forgive."

Ukrainian youth culture has signaled deep transformations within the country since independence more than three decades ago. Musicians have voiced a growing identification with and commitment to Ukraine that transcends regional, linguistic, and ethnic divisions. Their popularity reflects a reality not always apparent in the country's politics. Ukraine is one country with a shared culture, Skofka says, with a story of resilience, resistance, and resolve. It's also a country that will neither forget nor forgive.

8: Responsible Critical Citizenship through Art

May 17, 2024

Nikita Kadan's exhibit *The Ray Penetrates the Soil* at Kyiv's Voloshyn Gallery in March might seem, at first hearing, to have been a paradigmatic Ukrainian art show. As classic a Ukrainian theme as sun and soil might appear, however, Kadan's work was startlingly new. Consisting of several highly refined metal installations of stark simplicity, the artist's work simultaneously projected a traditional theme and stunningly contemporary abstraction.

Kadan's show, as all his work, combined reassuring comfort with unexpected abstraction. A child of a newly independent Ukraine, the artist, now 40-something, has exhibited at leading museums, fairs, and galleries around the world for over two decades. After graduating from the National Academy of Fine Art in Kyiv in 2007, Kadan began working with historians, architects, and human rights activists to establish the noteworthy R.E.P. (Revolutionary Experimental Space) Group during the 2004 Orange Revolution. He continued working with artists of his generation to define what it means to be free and to be Ukrainian in the 21st century. His appearance at the 2015 Venice Biennale cemented his standing as one of his generation's leading artists worldwide, not just in Ukraine.

This year's exhibit at the Voloshyn Gallery builds on his earlier wartime series "The Shadow on the Ground," which he developed while working in a bomb shelter. Drawing on what Kadan calls "poetics of visible evidence," that project emerged around the theme of Ukrainian black arable land. Seeing the damage left by a Russian missile hitting Shevchenko Park in Kyiv prompted his probe of Ukraine's fate through the image of its land. His astonishingly simple abstract sculptures, charcoal drawings, and paintings in this spring's exhibit captured the ways in which the war's intrusions leave lasting wounds on the landscape, a landscape deeply connected to an injured Ukraine.

His work shares a mission with the gallery to showcase Ukraine's most contemporary art. Founded in 2016, shortly after *Forbes Magazine* placed founders Max and Julia Voloshyn on its "30 Under 30" list of people to watch, the gallery has sought the integration of Ukrainian art with global cultural trends. Partnering with institutions and contemporary art fairs around the world, the Voloshyn Gallery has become a bridge between the Ukrainian and global contemporary artistic communities. For nearly a decade, the Voloshyns have brought the works of scores of leading contemporary Ukrainian artists to the attention of the international art world.

The Voloshyns closed their cutting-edge gallery, located in the basement of a century-old building on Tereshchenkivska Street overlooking Kyiv's Shevchenko Park, when the Russians launched their full-scale invasion. Within the year, they decamped for Miami's vibrant Wynwood district, bringing new Ukrainian works to the trendy South Florida art scene. As the couple told the German website ART COLOGNE, "Ukraine has a strong artistic voice, and for this reason, our mission is to keep moving. We want to make this voice be heard and welcomed in the world community."

They reopened their Kyiv gallery in mid-2023, engaging the city's vivid art scene as the Ukrainian capital's arts community reopened, despite the hardships of war. The intent is to pick up where the gallery had left off.

In a 2022 interview with *ArtForum's* David Velasco, Kadan explained the need for continuity. "In a peaceful, or a relatively peaceful time," he explained, "I was not so interested in this aspect of just being Ukrainian.... If we postpone criticalities for all of this period, we will turn to like basically an undemocratic state, you know?" He said, "No, we cannot postpone criticality, but we have to be responsible and make a proper practical solution." Kadan does so through his art. It's an artistic expression that remains rooted in Ukraine's black soil while simultaneously drawing on the most cutting-edge forms of contemporary artistic expression.

9: Kyiv Chamber Musicians Use Music to Lift Hearts High

May 24, 2024

Little in the world of classical music is more of a cliché than playing Vivaldi's *Four Seasons* in April to mark the beginning of spring (except, perhaps, a performance of the *Nutcracker* by an American ballet company in December). A musical revelation when first performed in Venice around 1720, the four concertos, written to accompany four sonnets charting the seasons, have become among the most (over)performed pieces in the history of classical music. Nonetheless, there is little cliché about playing this delightful suite in a city at war, as the National Chamber Ensemble Kyiv Soloists did in April at the Ukrainian capital's Freedom Hall.

Founded by virtuoso violinist Bohodar Kotorovych 25 years ago, the Kyiv Soloists have become one of the city's cultural gems. Kotorovych reached out to bring together Ukrainian musicians who have won various national and international competitions to showcase Ukrainian composers outside of Ukraine and international composers within Ukraine. The group continued after the founder's death in 2009. Anatoli Vasyokovski became artistic director in 2017.

Since its founding, the ensemble has promoted a variety of styles, bringing top Ukrainian performers together with visiting international stars, such as pianist Claudio Martinez Mehner from Spain, jazz singer Nino Katamadze from Georgia, Deep Purple founder Jon Lord from England, and jazz pianist Konstanty Wileński from Poland. This eclectic mix of classical and nonclassical genres led to successful tours in Austria, France, Germany, Singapore, and many other countries over the past quarter century. The group's reputation came to rest on founder Kotorovych's maxim, "Many orchestras possess skill, but not every orchestra lifts your hearts high."

The ensemble had just left Ukraine for a tour of Italy in February 2022 when the Russians launched their full-scale invasion.

Many in the group had family members in Ukraine and the group debated how best to proceed. Eventually, they decided to use their concerts to raise funds for the Ukraine war effort and continued their European "tour of pain." Their Italian promoter added several unscheduled concerts within Italy and helped the group garner media attention for themselves and for Ukraine. Concerts in Switzerland and Germany followed, with a program including works by Ukrainian composers Valentin Silvestrov, Maxim Berezovsky, and Aleksandr Shymko. King Gustav and Queen Silvia of Sweden attend a televised performance in Stockholm where they were joined by pianist Benny Andersson of ABBA.

By mid-2022, the ensemble had begun performing in Kyiv again, coming together for concerts at several different venues. Lifting hearts high took on new meaning as the war with Russia unfolded. The group performed as often as possible in Kyiv, despite ongoing threats of aerial attack (which at times prompted mid-concert blackouts). As in the past, the group moved among venues, including classical concert halls and churches.

The April performances of Vivaldi at Freedom Hall, near Kyiv's riverside neighborhood of Podil, represents the sort of nontraditional venue Kyiv Soloists have found attractive for reaching new classical audiences. The Freedom Hall Cultural Center opened its doors in 1994 and was renovated in 2018. A commercial center, it has hosted concerts ranging from classical music to rock, provided space for conferences and meetings, and reached out to its surrounding community as a cultural resource.

The ensemble performed other concerts in April, but the familiarity of Vivaldi's *Four Seasons* captured a need for classical comfort music amid the uncertainties of Russian attacks. These concertos signal the end of another harsh winter and the opening possibilities of spring, at a moment when Kyiv needs nothing more than to be reassured that life continues.

10: Warrior Princess and Poet Oksana Rubaniak Gives Voice to Her Generation's Anguish

May 31, 2024

Ukraine's red-haired warrior princess Oksana "Xena" Rubaniak was a natural subject for the Ukrainian edition of *Vogue* magazine to feature in a recent photo essay on how the war has changed the country. British photographer Brett Lloyd photographed Rubaniak in her military gear last February, along with other soldiers and model Karyna Mazyar. A 21-year-old poet and machine gunner, Rubaniak has established herself as a generational icon.

Social media had spread the word about Rubaniak before *Vogue*'s editors pointed Lloyd her way. Her good looks made her a natural symbol of a generation whose lives have been interrupted by war. Intending to become a primary school teacher upon graduating with honors from the Ivano-Frankivsk Vocational College at 19, Rubaniak changed course and started pursuing a degree in public administration and worked for the Youth Policy and Sports Department of the Ivano-Frankivsk City Council.

The full-scale Russian invasion put her plans and dreams on hold, as it did everyone in her generation. Rubaniak immediately enlisted in the Ukrainian military, rising to the rank of junior sergeant. At the time, she was the only woman in the machine gun platoon of the Black Zaporizhzhians 72nd Mechanized Brigade, which saw intense combat in Zaitseve, Bakhmut, Maryan, and Vuhledar. Seriously wounded in March 2022, she returned to the front that June and, earlier this year, became a platoon commander of the Armed Forces of Ukraine.

A native of the small village of Hramotne in the Ivano-Frankivsk region, Rubaniak long aspired to become a poet of note. Her first book of verse, *Ornaments of Fate* (2020), was published when she turned 19 and reveals a serious-minded young woman navigating from village childhood to urban adulthood. Her poems reflect a preoccupation with the meaning of life, the infinite repetition of ornamental patterns through human history, and the eternal challenges of frank honesty with oneself.

Her second book, *Toward Death* (2022), delves deeper into doubts about the meaning of life, with verses shaped by her experiences in battle. Once again, Rubaniak gives expression to her generation's loss of innocence and normalcy. Her poems speak for those who are struggling to come to terms with the collapse of hopeful plans.

Speaking to the UkraineWorld website in May 2023, Rubaniak says, "Many of my friends are gone." She continues: "And where are your friends? They are walking, studying, and working. Mine were killed in battle with the enemy, while others are still fighting for their right to live every day. My fallen friends and I meet not in cafes, parks, or restaurants, but in the cemeteries."

Indeed, she fears for a future in which the heroic act of fighting may become a fault. With the wisdom of a poet as well as a warrior, she says that veterans "will face disrespect, injustice, and disorder. We will need to learn to coexist, not to blame, not to insult each other, but to coexist."

Rubaniak continues to make her own plans for peacetime, even as she recognizes that her own death could be imminent. She looks forward to a day when she can return to writing as a primary vocation, speaking for her fellow Ukrainian 20-year-olds as they try to recover dreams that once felt promised.

11: Bringing the Light of Jerusalem to Ukraine

June 7, 2024

March was a time of turmoil for those who identify as being both Ukrainian and Jewish. The war with Russia in Ukraine and the ongoing fighting in the Middle East heightened passions around what it means to be either. Or both. An exhibit in Chernivtsi, *The Light of Jerusalem,* embraces the city's Jewish past as part of its present.

Throughout the month, hundreds of viewers made their way to that city's Vernissage Centre of Culture to visit an exhibition of paintings and modern graphics by established Ukrainian artist Natalia Korobova. Speaking at the opening reception, Chief Rabbi Menachem Mendel Glitzenstein congratulated the artist on combining "material mastery" of technique with penetrating spirituality.

Chernivtsi—formerly known as Czernowitz—has long been at the center of the region's conflicting identities. Romanian, Russian, German, Polish, and Ukrainian forces fought over the city with the collapse of the Hapsburg Empire following World War I. Ceded to Romania during the interwar period, the city became a focal point of Jewish intellectual life. Tragically, more than half of the region's Jewish population perished in the Holocaust. Soviet authorities largely ignored this Jewish history, putting various Jewish religious and community buildings to secular use. Postindependence cultural institutions, including the Vernissage Centre, have highlighted the region's Jewish cultural heritage through exhibitions such as Korobova's, as well as lectures, concerts, and various performances celebrating Jewish holidays.

Korobova has enjoyed a varied and successful career for more than 50 years. The daughter of the well-known Zaporizhzhia landscape and figurative painter Vladimir Korobov, she exhibited around the Soviet Union and abroad during the 1970s and 1980s. She took a break from painting to work as a clown. With Ukrainian independence, she worked as a magazine editor and collaborated with the Zaporizhzhia publisher Wild Field, gaining recognition as an illustrator. If she became known as a successful portrait painter early in her career, over the past quarter century her work has connected realism with lyricism.

As Rabbi Glitzenstein noted at the exhibition's opening, her watercolors and oil paintings—including landscapes, cityscapes, and portraits exploring the special light of Jerusalem—blend her fascination with physical detail and metaphysical wonderment. Their bright gracefulness lifts viewers out of the present moment, making the exhibit an antidote to the travails of war.

An exhibition of Ukrainian Easter traditions followed Korobkova's show. Master musicians and dance students joined in concert to celebrate the long-anticipated arrival of spring. Another show, a few weeks later, showed the works of 40 children in different styles and disciplines. Each new show puts a spotlight on another aspect of the region's complex multicultural heritage and its present. Together, they draw on what is positive from the past to point to a future of creativity.

Chernivtsi's Vernissage Cultural Center has opened its doors throughout the current war with Russia to convene community groups through the arts. The center's concerts, dance performances, and art exhibitions have offered respite from the strains of war. They have embraced the multiplicity of identities that have shaped the region's tragic history. Located at the crossroads of Europe's heart of 20th century darkness, the city has experienced multiple horrors: more than a century of war, ethnic cleansing, religious intolerance, and political divides.

12: Finding Light on Stage in Dark Times

June 14, 2024

Theater director Anatoliy Levchanko resurrected the Mariupol Drama Theatre in Kyiv in April. The company staged a performance of Neda Nezhdana's *Light at the End of the Tunnel* at the Les Kurbas Centre in a remarkable feat of resilience, since its stately building is gone.

Levchenko had been scheduled to open a new production at his Mariupol theater the day after the Russians launched their full-scale invasion in February 2022. Instead, the city and his theater were brutalized as Russian forces came to occupy the port city in a cyclone of violence captured by Stystav Chernov's Oscar-winning documentary *20 Days in Mariupol*. The theater was obliterated a couple of weeks later by Russian rockets, slaughtering up to 600 civilians (including several hundred children) who mistakenly thought there would be no attack on a cultural landmark with "Children" spelled out in large letters on its roof.

Levchenko's travails were only beginning. The Russians captured him and imprisoned him in Donetsk for 10 months on suspicion of terrorism without bringing any charges. Once released, Levchenko and his family made their way across battle lines to Ukrainian-controlled territory. Settling in Kyiv with his wife and son, Levchenko set about reviving his company.

Controversy was not new to Levchenko's dramaturgy. He assumed the directorship of the Mariupol Drama Theatre in 1994 and set out to revive the company along European—rather than Soviet—models. In 2020, authorities refused to renew his contract, citing his embrace of what they saw as "pro-Ukrainian" artistic and political programs. He established his own company, Terra Incognita, to stage Ukrainian and Russian plays as well as works from abroad.

Once in exile in Kyiv, Levchenko found it difficult to pull his actors together. Some members of his company had found safer haven in western Ukraine, where they brought their wartime experiences to the stage. Others remained under Russian occupation, performing for the new authorities and decrying the purported abuses of Ukrainian nationalists. Eventually, Levchenko assembled a cast comprised primarily of Mariupol drama students who had managed to relocate to Kyiv.

Levchenko chose Neda Nezhdana's *Light at the End of the Tunnel* as his reconstituted company's first offering. Nezhdana's one-act satire revolves around two women trapped in an underground morgue, which symbolizes the collapsing Soviet Union. Eventually they realize that they have been confined for no particular reason and are free to leave. For playwright Nezhdana, the new production reveals how a work she thought of engaging one historic event—the collapse of the Soviet Union—now speaks to the challenges of a second, the current war.

The company's return to the stage assumed special meaning for the thousands of refugees from Mariupol who have relocated to Kyiv. Temporary extra seating was added opening night to accommodate all of the Mariupolites who wanted to attend. The evening connected those who had been forced from their homes to one another and to their new city in fresh ways. As one audience member who had fled occupation told Anna Malpas from the website Barron's, "It's like we lost something there and it's been moved here. It gives me goosebumps." Finding so many others who have shared the experience of exile strengthened their resolve to resist Russian aggression.

Beyond any artistic achievement, Levchenko's production underscores the continuing determination of many Ukrainians to carry on as regular a life as possible despite the war. The director, cast, and audience members joined to continue what they had begun prior to February 2022: to engage with theater as a way of understanding the present. The light at the end of Nezhdana's imagined tunnel shines as bright as ever.

13: Stolen Spring but Not Stolen Humanity

June 21, 2024

Photographer Olena Grom has been fleeing Russian invaders for nearly a decade. Born in Donetsk, she trained and developed her technique in and around her native city. Hoping to have a career as a conceptual artist, she discovered that photography empowered her creative instincts. She quickly gained a national and international reputation, earning exhibitions and recognition as far away as Singapore, Colombia, and Canada. Then Putin's "little green men" entered her hometown and, with local collaborators, proclaimed it to be part of Russia.

Grom and her family made their way west, eventually settling in the Kyiv suburb Bucha, and she set up a studio in neighboring Irpin. Her professional achievements continued, with opportunities to show her work in Kyiv as well as in galleries across Europe. Her career flourished. International photography juries began recognizing her work. Bucha and Irpin seemed a safe haven for Grom to pursue her creative life.

But Bucha, it turned out, was on the Russian route to Kyiv. In February 2022, she and her neighbors stood in the way of a full-scale invasion. They would soon suffer almost total destruction, massacres and other unspeakable war crimes.

Grom managed to leave Bucha briefly, only to return after the Russians pulled out weeks later. Complete devastation and profound trauma became her reality as she and her neighbors began rebuilding their communities and personal lives as best they could. As she surveyed her town, she began to think about Michael Nash's photographs of the complete destruction of Warsaw at the end of World War II. Nash's work inspired Grom to turn her camera on the devastation surrounding her.

As she began taking her photos, Grom noted that those who had survived were too preoccupied with reconstructing their lives to notice that spring had arrived. Flowers blossomed amidst the rubble; birds flew in from their winter travels. Nature reaffirmed life in ways beyond human capacity. She hit upon the idea of contrasting the Russian destruction with nature's rebirth.

Grom created studio-sized photographic backdrops showing spring scenes—bright flowers, babbling brooks, open fields—and set them up outside in front of the blackened, war-ruined urban landscape that had become Bucha's reality. She invited neighbors to don their best remaining clothing and pose in front of her camera. The result is "Stolen Spring," a series of portraits revealing both the horror of physical ruin and the hopes of spring and of her resilient neighbors who were setting out to rebuild their town. This project became her psychological salvation even as she, her family, friends, and neighbors confronted some of the worst horrors of 21st century war.

Two years on, her powerful photographs have made their way out of Bucha via the internet and exhibitions around the world. The 15 international jurors of the annual Fine Art Photography Awards (FAPA) were among those admiring Grom's work. They awarded her twice during this year's competition, once as Professional Photographer of the Year, and also with first place in the Professional Portrait category.

For the past decade, FAPA has become one of the world's leading awards programs. FAPA asks its jury to honor "artists and unique souls who breathe and live for creativity." The awards have encouraged photographers to define their own personal vision for their work, eschewing technique and strictures of form. Grom's gripping images combining human dignity, the hope of spring, and the terror of war represented FAPA's goals.

Humanity often is lost as war grinds on. Grom's photography from Bucha and Irpin reveals that neither humankind nor nature disappear. A future with hope may be found in the sanctuaries of peace and springtime.

14: A Darkness of Interest

June 28, 2024

The 2022 Russian invasion seemingly brought an end to bestselling author Illarion Pavliuk's literary career. The writer re-enlisted in the armed forces and, over the past two years, moved from the battlefield to senior positions in the Ministry of Defense. More recently, he became the leader of the Main Intelligence Directorate's Press and Information Department.

Lviv's Old Lion Publishing House released Pavliuk's *I See You Are Interested in Darkness* in 2020. When his novel came out, many reviewers immediately drew parallels between Pavliuk's work and the novels of American Stephen King. Both reveal evil's continuously grinding assault on human kindness in ways which transgress the boundaries of reality. The darkness described in Pavliuk's 639-page noir detective story seems ever present during Ukraine's wartime struggles. These connections between fiction and reality probably explain the novel's continuing bestseller status.

The novel is both deeply embedded in Ukraine and reminiscent of stories found elsewhere. Pavliuk's detective hero Andri Gaister arrives in a small village, Buskiv Sad, to help local authorities find a missing girl, Nadya. Gaister quickly realizes that there is much more happening in what seems to be an idyllic village. As he asks around, he learns that a serial killer—the Beast—has been mutilating women's bodies. Moreover, he realizes that "the Beast" might not even exist. But if not, who is perpetrating this bloodshed? The more he looks for the culprit behind these mysterious brutalities, the more he comes to see fear and impenetrable indifference at the heart of human darkness. Evil thrives in the dark spaces left.

War leaves little room for indifference and ignorance. The 2022 Russian invasion has forced all Ukrainians to examine what matters to them, and to determine how they will respond. Unlike the denizens of Pavliuk's Buskiv Sad, contemporary real-life Ukrainians have brought as much light to bear on the evil attacking them as they can. *I See You Are Interested in Darkness* offers a guide to how to engage one's personal sins, and society's failings and capabilities.

Ukrainian readers knew Pavliuk before his current position and his latest bestseller. Born in the Kherson region a decade before Ukrainian independence, he and his parents moved to Sakhalin in the Russian Far East for most of his teenage years. He returned to Ukraine and settled in Luhansk, where he earned a university degree in journalism. He moved to Kyiv and started a successful television career, initially as an international journalist covering the Arab-Israeli conflict. He later became editor in chief at TV channel K1 and moved on to direct the 2007 Documentary Film Studio. In 2015, he volunteered to fight against Russian aggression in the Donbas.

Pavliuk eventually settled with his family in Ivano-Frankivsk, where he launched a documentary film studio as well as a community-oriented nongovernmental organization. He published his first novel, *White Ashes*, in 2018, followed by a Christmas anthology and a space adventure novel. The appearance of *I See You Are Interested in Darkness* in 2020 took his writing career to new heights.

Darkness pervades Pavliuk's writing, television recording, and documentary films. Spending time in Israel, Gaza, and the West Bank ended any illusions about human nature. The experiences in an independent Ukraine struggling to secure its place in the world amplified his sense of the shadows within the human spirit. His opposition to Russia's claims to Ukraine demolished whatever connections he had to the country of his adolescence. The Devil has always been a local call away, throughout each chapter of his biography. His acute appreciation of the destructiveness of indifference became further refined until it spilled out on the pages of his massive novel.

Pavliuk captures widespread contradictions and ambiguities in Ukrainian life and human existence, opacities which mark the uncertainties of postindependence Ukraine. The continuing popularity of his novel reveals how many Ukrainians share his interest in darkness. After 2022, indifference was no longer an option for its readers.

15: Odesa: More of a Ukrainian Past than Before 2022

July 12, 2024

Since its founding by Catherine the Great in 1794 as an outpost of her empire, Odesa has been a multicultural entrepôt, bringing together people from all over. Once among the Russian Empire's largest cities and most important ports, Odesa lost some of its aura following World War II. Nonetheless, sailors from around the world continued to call out "Odesa Mama" whenever they came to call.

Odesa regained its maritime importance following Ukrainian independence, as the new country's largest port. The city became home to large number of immigrant traders from Africa and Central and South Asia throughout the 1990s into the early 2000s. National customs and local police authorities exercised only limited control over the sprawling informal markets outside of town. The city has always welcomed all sorts of people and continued to do so into its third century.

Russian remained the city's lingua franca, and Ukrainians remained a distinct minority in a town dominated at various times by Russian, Greek, Italian, Polish, and Jewish settlers. Present-day Russians interpreted the city's multicultural realities to mean that the town should be theirs. Present-day Ukrainians admit to feeling, at times, that it was not quite Ukrainian. All of this changed with the Russian full-scale invasion of 2022.

For more than two years, Russian artillery and rockets have rained down on Odesa with destructive regularity. These barrages have solidified local—and national—identities as Ukrainian. Odesa now overflows with Ukrainian patriots. Claiming the city as their own, many are discovering that their town has had deep ties to Ukrainian culture all along.

For example, the Odesa Literature Museum, founded a half-century ago in the former Sikar Mansion, is a remarkable institution that continues to uncover deep Ukrainian linkages to local urban culture. The Russian poet Aleksandr Pushkin stayed in the building in 1823 when it was Hotel du Nord, a connection which has been celebrated with the museum attaching Pushkin's name to its own.

Throughout its history, the museum has gathered artifacts and archives related to writers in several languages who have been born, worked, or sojourned in the city. These collections support various exhibits, lectures, concerts, and publication efforts that appropriately proclaim Odesa as a leading global literary hot spot. The museum's heroic staff has kept it open throughout much of the past two years, even as Russian shelling has damaged its facilities.

This spring, the museum mounted a major exhibition of works by and about Ukraine's national bard Taras Shevchenko, highlighting connections with Odesa. These artifacts, selected to honor the 210th anniversary of Shevchenko's birth into serfdom, included first editions dating from the 19th century about his life, his artwork (he was a painter as well as a poet), and his importance for Ukraine. Correspondence between Shevchenko, who had been exiled to the Orsk Fortress in the Urals because of his expressions of Ukrainian nationalism, and Odesan writer Andrii Lyzogub offers insight into Shevchenko's travails while incarcerated.

Up to now, Shevchenko's ties to Odesa often received scant attention in comparison to the city's place in the lives of prominent Russian and Jewish authors. By mounting this exhibition, the museum casts light on the city's too-often-ignored role in the emergence of a Ukrainian literary canon. The exhibit is an example of a recalibration of identity that has been playing out throughout Ukraine since the 2022 Russian invasion.

Ukrainians of all backgrounds are reexamining who they are and who they are not. Once-ignored connections to the country's past assume new meaning; urban cultures associated with Russia appear to have long-standing connections with Ukraine. Ukrainians are not reinventing a past that suits the moment. Rather, they are discovering a past that was always there but submerged under broader imperial, Soviet, and Russian chronicles. As the Odesa Literature Museum shows, Odesa will be Ukrainian after this war has ended in part because it always has been.

16: Theater—Not Bread—Lines in Kyiv

July 19, 2024

Bread or some other pantry staple might seem to await those patient souls standing in a three-hour long queue during the height of a war. In Kyiv, this spring, it was theater.

For months, director Ivan Urovsky's production of Hryhoriy Kvitka-Osnovyanenko's novel *The Witches of Konop* has sold out at Kyiv's venerable Ivan Franko National Drama Theater. The lines have taken over nearby streets as early as 5 a.m., in part because of wartime restrictions on the frequency of shows. The lines have grown as theater management stopped making seats available online, to counteract the large number of fraudulent tickets being resold at exorbitant prices. Old-fashioned trips to the box office are the only way to buy a legitimate coupon to gain entrance.

Ticket demand has run high ever since the play's premier a year ago. Director Urovsky, artist Tetiana Ovsiychuk, and choirmaster Susanna Karpenko each have won prestigious Shevchenko Prizes for their work. And *The Witches* has won the war-weary city's heart.

Urovsky's adaptation is but the latest take on a nearly two-century-old story of Cossacks, misplaced witch hunts, and tortured love. Author Kvitka was born in 1778 in the village of Osnova, which is today within the Kharkiv city limits. By century's end, he became a writer and one of the earliest proponents of Ukrainian as a literary language. As his career took shape, he added "Osnovyanenko" to his pen name to mark his ties to his birthplace.

By 1812, Kvitka had become the editor of one of the first literary journals published in Ukrainian, and the director of a new theater in Kharkiv. His satirical novels and plays—including *Marusia,* one of the first novellas in Ukrainian—attracted readers and audiences to his work. His *Visitor from the Capitol or Turmoil in a District Town* is said to have inspired his friend Mykola Hohol (Nikolai Gogol) to pen his famous *Government Inspector. The Witches of Konop* appeared as Kvitka's second book, in 1837, though it had been written four years earlier.

Witches tells the story of Nikiya Ulasovich Zabryokha, the local Cossack leader in Konotop, his clerk Pistryak, and the witch Yavdokha Zubikha. The convoluted story of intrigue revolves around Cossack troops, failed love, *faux* bravery, and a search for the witch, who is preventing rain from falling on the village.

Hoping to attract rain clouds, authorities bound local women and threw them into a nearby pond. If they died, they were innocent; if they floated, they were witches. Zubikha survived, and the locals began to beat her up. Zabryokha saved her and asked her, in return, to make an unrequited love marry him. The witch did so but cast a spell over the couple so that their marriage would be an unhappy one. After several more twists and turns, everyone dies.

Full of moments open to conflicting interpretation, this tale has inspired films, numerous stage adaptations, and even a popular 2016 rap tune. Every Ukrainian knows the story's general contours, which opens opportunities for ever more creative reinterpretations and dramatic stagings. Urovsky's modernist setting at the Ivan Franko provides a startling counterpart to a story that is premodern in outlook but which feels fresh.

A popular social media video circulating just after the Russian full-scale invasion shows an old Ukrainian woman yelling at a young Russian tank driver attempting to make his way down her village's main street. "Don't you know where you are?" she cries. "You're in Konotop. Every other woman here is a witch." She then placed a curse on the invader, to ruin his love life.

17: Theater as Ukraine's Safe Space for Absorbing the Traumas of War

July 26, 2024

Ukrainian theater has emerged over the course of the past two years as an important public forum for airing the most sensitive issues arising from the full-scale Russian invasion in 2022. Scores of playwrights have written about their own experiences, producing new works which provide a vivid chronicle of Ukraine at war. Many of their scripts have been produced, both in Ukraine and abroad.

As theaters began to reopen under martial law strictures, their staging of new and old works provided both relief from the hardships of war and opportunities to nurture public dialogue about its displacements. Ukraine's collective and personal responses to war's traumas have been dramatically visible from its stages.

Iulia Bentia and Pavlo Shopin, two Ukrainian theater scholars, recently undertook a foray into what wartime theater reveals about their society's traumas, aspirations, and dispositions in an article in the journal *Art History in Ukraine* (*Mystetstvoznavstvo*). The authors turned for evidence to submissions made last year for the fifth All-Ukrainian Festival organized by the National Union of Theater Artists of Ukraine. Dating from 2017, the festival has presented productions by companies large and small, from every corner of the country. No festival took place in 2022, so the 2023 festival presented 134 performances staged in 2021 and 2022, ranging from plays for children to large-scale productions, from musicals to experimental works.

Eighteen of the plays related directly to the current war. These contemporary wartime works explored the challenges of emigration, tests of mental health, and a range of moral issues surrounding key questions of loyalty, violence, and the meaning of community.

Bentia and Shopin were particularly interested in how recent traumas of war have reshaped interpretations of classical theatrical works, and how those works empower audiences to think differently about their own daily travails. They examined four productions in particular: Ivan Franko Theater's stagings of Albert Camus's *Caligula* and Lesya Ukrainka's dramatic poem *Cassandra*; Theater on Podil's production of Sophocles's *Oedipus Rex*; and Poltava Puppet Theater's *The Great Dungeon*, based on Taras Shevchenko's "mystery poem." These productions reimagined classic theatrical works while considering current events, both shedding new insight into the works themselves and framing painful conversations about the dislocations of the current war.

The authors argued that theater provides a safe social space for public discussion seeking to understand the traumas imposed by the current war. *Caligula* raised penetrating insights into the brutality and immorality of authoritarian rule and contributed to media discussions about the mental health of the Russian president. *Oedipus* related to the growing demand for justice in wartime society at a time when discussions over morality are gaining in importance. *Cassandra* explored the ways in which humans protect themselves by constructing fanciful illusions. Shevchenko's work sets the current conflict against the backdrop of previous Russo-Ukrainian conflicts.

Bentia and Shopin conclude that each of the festival's productions—both those only two months old and those written two millennia ago—provided a safe space for emotional responses to shared tragedy. While acknowledging that the full-scale Russian invasion has attracted unprecedented attention to Ukrainian theater both at home and abroad, they are most interested in the social aspects of theater that help uncover how Ukrainians understand and overcome the traumatic experiences of war.

"The Ukrainian theater," they write, "actively responds to the new reality, participates in various ways in relevant public discussions that try to understand the drama of modern war, and creates a safe space for common emotional reliving a new tragic experience." Their article shows the ways in which live theater still delivers support for communities at times of distress.

18: Extending the Ukrainian New Wave Into a New Era

August 2, 2024

Alexander Roitburd changed the course of Ukrainian contemporary art as a painter, installation artist, videographer, photographer, and organizer. A founder of the Ukrainian New Wave of the 1990s and a theorist within the Ukrainian Transavantgard, his influence continues to shape the art world, even after his 2021 death. A continuing exhibit at the Odesa Fine Arts Museum tells the story of Roitburd's artistry and influence, even as the institution struggles with the exigencies of war.

Roitburd graduated from the Odesa Pedagogical Institute in 1983 and seized the opportunities emerging during the Gorbachev years to experiment with art forms that moved beyond the staid markers of the Soviet period. Ukrainian independence accelerated his embrace of post-Soviet postmodernism. In 1993, he co-founded the New Art Association in Odesa and remained in its leadership until the early 2000s. His provocative works won spots at major galleries and museums in Ukraine, Russia, Europe, and North America.

His distinctive, highly stylized art works merged elements of the surreal with more organic forms, often with a flavor of irony. Images emerge from the canvas as hints of more representational images. Kyryll Lipatov, the curator of the exhibit, writes on the museum's website, "Lines multiply and become confused. Lines weaken and sag. Lines stretch and tremble. The lines are sprinkled with dots. Lines disappear into the horizon. Lines line up in azimuths. Overripe friendships are divided by borders. Lines are tightened with a loop. They rub against each other, sprinkling rosin; the lines sing. Holes in the canvas are filled with allusions."

Roitburd's role as a leader of what has become known as the Ukrainian New Wave helped set Ukrainian contemporary art off in new directions following independence. The movement emerged during perestroika, as young artists of his generation (those born in the 1960s) broke away from the suffocating embrace of Soviet officialdom. They sought to make personal statements with their art, drawing on what they were seeing in the avant-garde and postmodernist movements of the West that had been closed to them by Soviet censorship.

The artists of this generation never embraced a single vision, but they shared common interests in the promotion of creative freedom, individual independence, and experimentation. These are characteristics marking Roitburd's work and are features of the art he promoted in his various organizational roles.

His own artistic sensibility reflected the city of his birth. Odesa long has been a place where the supernatural and the absurd can seem normal, where a sly humor always lurks just beneath life's surface. It is a sensibility which won him fans beyond Odesa, and yet it is in his hometown where he remains most appreciated. Just two months before he died of cancer at age 59, he established a program supporting art chronicling contemporary artistic development in the city and throughout Ukraine. At last count, these funds have enabled his hometown's museum to add 670 new works to its collection.

The museum's continuing display of Roitburd's work is a reminder of the autonomous development of Ukrainian cultural life cut short by the 2022 Russian full-scale invasion. Its continuation reflects a determination to draw fresh sustenance from his oeuvre, even as Russian weapons inflict harm on Ukrainian cultural institutions. Once the last bomb has fallen, Ukrainians will resume their own artistic trajectories. Thanks to the work of institutions such as the Odesa Fine Arts Museum—with its exhibitions of Roitburd's work and the hundreds of new works his funding has made possible—much will be available to inspire new directions in Ukrainian art.

19: Loving Kyiv's Legends

August 6, 2024

The current war has cemented many Ukrainians' love affairs with their hometowns. The more Russian missiles rain down on Kharkiv, Odesa, and Kyiv, the stronger the attachment their residents feel toward where they live. Even Kyiv, thought of as an aloof capital by many, has become an object of affection. The May premiere of Catherine Penkova's *Legends of Kyiv* at the Theater of Drama and Comedy on the Left Bank captured this love.

Penkova's play, directed by Natalia Sivanenko, tells the stories of many historical events and beloved personages across more than a thousand years of the city's history. The family-friendly play brings history and fictional tales to life as it connects otherwise scattered incidents into a single tapestry. The theater pulled together a dozen actors from its own company as well as other Kyiv theaters to remind viewers that Kyiv can be, and should be, loved despite the current hardships.

The Theater on the Left Bank has a rich history. The troupe was organized in 1978 and produced its first offering a few months later downtown at the Republic Puppet Theater (now the Brodsky Choral Synagogue). The company moved around until the city government turned the former customs building and Cosmos Cinema on the Dnipro's left bank over to Eduard Mytynsky to run as the "Theater in the Lobby." The current company took shape with Ukrainian independence and began presenting up to 50 performances a year. Ukrainian language productions steadily replaced Russian language plays following independence.

Known for small, topical plays during the late Soviet era, the theater was given more leeway than more prominent companies. From time to time, the company would insert contemporary works into its repertoire of classical drama. Its diminutive size and out-of-the-way location attracted some of Kyiv's top actors of the era who were searching for more modern—and pointed—works, since Soviet cultural bosses found small, hidden-away venues less threatening.

The company embraced contemporary, topical drama as soon as the fetters of Soviet censorship came off. Company directors Stas Zhyrkov and Tamara Trunova made the theater a seat of social and political commentary following their joint appointments in 2019. Olesya Zhurakivska became artistic director in 2023.

In March 2022, the company premiered Tamara Trunova's award-winning production of Natalia Vorozhbyt's powerful play *Bad Roads*. This work tells the stories of shattered roads and relationships in Donbas after Russia claimed the area as its own in 2014. As a sign of the times, the theater warned patrons that, in addition to sounds of shelling and explosions, some of the characters speak Russian and sing Russian songs. This bilingualism, the warning added, corresponds to the linguistic realities of Eastern Ukraine at the time.

The theater's left-bank location has shaped its feisty reputation. Located on Brovarskyi Prospekt across the street from the Circle Line's Livoberezhna station, the theater forces audience members to search it out, just as audiences would when heading to London's South Bank or New York's Brooklyn. Opposite the hilly historic city center on the other side of the river, the flat left bank has remained something of an afterthought. Soviet-era housing construction turned the area into one of the city's most populous areas, as housing block after housing block sprang to life like mushrooms after rain.

Like the South Bank and Brooklyn, this area remained "the wrong side of the river" to many. But, just as for its London and New York counterparts, this perception has begun to change. As *Legends of Kyiv* shows, Kyivans have come to love their city, even its less distinguished locations, and left-bank Kyiv no longer seems quite so culturally distant.

20: How to Stop Living Poetry and Start Living a New Reality

August 16, 2024

Ironic rock band Smetana (Sour Cream) has brought its distinctive mix of punk, pop, and alternative rock to audiences throughout wartime Ukraine on a spring-long tour. The group, which burst out of Dnipro in 2013, has enjoyed popularity for more than a decade. Adept at leveraging social media to attract a following, Smetana's mix of irony, commentary, and hard rock instrumentation spoke to the era's disappointments, failed dreams, and illusions. Since the Russian full-scale invasion in 2022, it also speaks to its generation's hopes for the future.

Singer Yehor Kuvaldin, guitarist Serhii Savockhin, bassist Oleksandr Sadunenko, and Serhiy Svergun formed the band as a joke to showcase songs which did not fit into the repertoire of their heavy metal group All Is Illusion. Shading towards more popular sounds accompanied by lighter, humorous lyrics, the new group quickly expanded its following. Smetana's first four albums—including *Worse than Last* and *They Don't Need Rock*—mocked trends in popular culture and music. More and more listeners embraced their parodies as speaking to the dissatisfactions of growing up in a Ukraine that seemed more of a failure than a success.

Kuvaldin and his bandmates continued to work on their metal performances which, to them, seemed more serious. In 2017, their fifth album as Smetana, *Everything Is Bad,* broke through as its music video went viral on social media. By 2020, the group was hitting the top of several music charts even as it avoided cultivating mainstream media. Smetana was, up until this point, a Russian-language alternative rock group enjoying social media success and attracting large audiences to its live performances. The Russian invasion of 2022 changed everything.

The band immediately supported Ukraine following the 2022 attack. It stopped singing in Russian and switched to Ukrainian, held charity concerts to support the armed forces, and released a powerful new single, "A Moment of Silence." This effort was followed by several more singles a few months later.

Just before releasing these songs and others on an album, Kuvaldin recorded a video message for the band's fans. He explained that he no longer wanted to release songs in Russian, even though abandoning his mother tongue was difficult personally, professionally, and artistically. As he would sing, "A third of the listeners turned into enemies / A third branded us traitors / And this means that only ours are left." This last third turned out to form a substantial and committed fan base living through the same pressures, frustrations, and hardships of war.

The group's next album appeared in August 2023 as its first Ukrainian-language production combining pop punk, alternative, post-punk, and hip-hop. Shortly thereafter, it released a collection of Ukrainian translations of the group's Russian-language hits under the title *Bad Vodka.*

The music featured in Smetana's recent all-Ukraine tour drew on these wartime albums (2023, 2024). Early on, the bandmates worried about their success, singing, "How to stop thinking in poetry and start living?" But war has converted their poetry into real life, as their recent success reflects skill at speaking to Ukraine's current crisis with wisdom disguised as humor.

The band came into existence a decade ago to mock the status quo of a Ukraine that seemed not to know any future. Ukraine's future, though hardly clear now, has become far more important to the generation coming of age with Smetana. This is a time, and the band's music is a sound, that continues to embrace sly humor even as it recognizes that the stakes placed on the table by Russian invaders have never been higher.

21: Art Defending the Right of Ukrainians to Choose Their Own Destinies

September 6, 2024

Washington area art lovers have had ample opportunity in recent weeks to view stunning and moving new works from wartime Ukraine at two consecutive shows. The first, *A Closer Look: Conflicted Art from Ukraine*, ran at George Mason University's Arlington exhibition gallery from May 31 through August 23. The second, *WKWTA* or *We Know Who They Are*, opened August 24 and runs through September 27 at Gallery 102 on the George Washington University campus, a few blocks from the State Department and the White House.

Together, the shows present several dozen new works by a score of artists. All produced since the full-scale Russian invasion in February 2022, the works use varied media and different genres, from lithographs, engravings, photographs, watercolors, acrylics, and oils to metal and wood sculptures and repurposed war artifacts. One large work, Andrey Datura's *Diplomatic Arrangement*, is painted in the artist's own blood.

The creators are well-known and amateur, young and established, and male and female. They are geographically dispersed. But they all turned to art to express their deepest emotional responses to the war. A partial list includes Natalya Amirova, Alexander Bondarchuk, Anatoliy Kvitka, Nata Levitasova, Olena Papka, Roman Rabyk, and Vitalij Zdebskij.

Their subjects range from images of widespread destruction and moments of savagery to touching moments of human contact and overwhelming sadness, both personal and public. The images immortalize genocidal slaughter at Bucha and Irpin, touching railway farewells, and resurgent life against shattered cityscapes. A few turn a sad, wistful look at what has been lost; others share a wry poke at Russian politicians and their soldiers. Their emotional power ranges from terror and outrage to feelings of kindness and nostalgia for the familiar comforts of home.

Virginia IT specialist Yevhen Nemchenko collected the works, beginning with the onset of the war (the very first air raid siren to be used in Kyiv is among the artifacts included in the *WKWTA* collection). Raised in Ukraine and in Russia, Nemchenko has relatives on both sides of the conflict.

Already collecting American art for a decade, he immediately understood the power of art at this moment. He reached out to friends and family in Ukraine to confirm that they were well. Then, he began acquiring art works being produced in response to the war. One purchase led to another, then another... His collection of several hundred items has become an invaluable historic record of the war and Ukraine's profound societal and cultural responses to it.

Nemchenko has worked with numerous partners, including co-curators Sophie Bae, George Mason University collections manager; and Benjamin Cunningham, a George Washington University political science and fine arts student. Cunningham has partnered with Nemchenko and his wife Kristina in building the Conflicted Art collection.

This cooperative work will not stop when the exhibition at George Washington University closes. A book containing works in both exhibitions is available online. Plans are afoot to take the shows to Philadelphia and Chicago, and to make them available for touring to other galleries. Several are for sale. Moreover, Nemchenko will continue to build his collection for as long as hostilities continue.

Gallery materials from both venues explain why this art is of vital importance. The show at George Washington University reminds viewers on its website that "the Ukrainian art scene is vibrant and that the people of Ukraine are suffering but have a resolute will to protect their right to live, be free, and choose their destiny." George Mason University's organizers struck a more universal theme, with, "Conflict is often perceived as a natural part of human existence, yet there is a critical need for more comprehensive efforts to prevent its escalation into violence."

The exhibits are a reminder of art's power to raise resolve to protect the ability of humans in Ukraine and elsewhere to choose their destiny; and our collective need to do all we can to prevent the escalation of conflict into violence everywhere.

22: Kharkiv Teaches Us That Theater Matters as Bombs Fall

September 13, 2024

Few Ukrainian cities have been as brutalized in recent months as Kharkiv. Just 30 kilometers from the border, Kharkiv has been savagely attacked for nearly three years, since the Russian full-scale invasion began. The Russian bombardment escalated earlier this summer as the Russians launched a new offensive. Hardly a block of the city has gone unscathed, with many landmark buildings suffering grievous damage.

Civil and military authorities, emergency personnel, and soldiers have defended the city heroically. Schools reopened underground to teach students, no matter how brutal the attacks above. The local fire department has emerged as particularly courageous. Simply continuing to live in the city has become a brave gesture.

Incredibly, the city's cultural life has persisted, even as more Russian bombs have fallen on it. Art shows, photo exhibits, classical music recitals, and chamber opera performances have continued, though in limited form. No one considered cancelling this year's Kharkiv Music Festival, the annual highlight of the city's classical music calendar. Bomb shelters, basements, and metro stations have served as arts venues in recent months as both performers and audience members continue to show up.

The city's century-old Kharkiv Shevchenko Ukrainian Drama Theater managed to offer a full summer season (though in a diminutive, makeshift, six-row hall). Live productions included Franz Kafka's *The Castle,* Albert Camus' *Caligula,* Neil Simon's *California Suite,* the Brothers Grimm's *Town Musicians of Bremen,* and Ukrainian classics such as Lesya Ukrainka's *Forest Song* and Mykola Kulish's *My Mausoleum.* The theater webcast many of these productions.

Today's Drama Theater is a descendent of the illustrious Berezil Theatre founded by Les Kurbas in 1922. That company moved to Kyiv after Ukraine's capital decamped from Kharkiv and was suppressed by the Soviet government during the 1930s. A new company took shape in Kharkiv out of the remnants of the earlier company. Further disruptions followed during World War II. The theater consolidated throughout the remainder of the Soviet era as a significant Ukrainian stage. The company came into its own following independence, especially under the artistic directorship of Andriy Zholdak in the early 2000s. Another cycle of political interference—this time over a controversial production of *Romeo and Juliet* in 2005—forced Zholdak to leave the theater for Germany.

Current Artistic Director Stepan Pasichnyk established himself as an actor, director, teacher, poet, and playwright during the years leading up to Ukrainian independence. Known for his philosophical bent, his work has appealed both to theater professionals as well as to large, youthful audiences. His leadership of the Shevchenko company has offered plentiful opportunity to experiment with blending realism and imagination. Like his company and hometown, Pasichnyk is a survivor.

The Drama Theater is one of many examples demonstrating how the war has energized the city's cultural life to transcend mere survival. Local puppet theater actor Nina Khyzhna told *The Guardian* that "doing theatre here makes so much more sense [than abroad]. The audience has heard the same explosions in the night, [and] their houses have shaken from the same shockwaves." She returned to Kharkiv from an artistic residency in Austria, finding the sense of safety she felt in Europe an illusion. The war offered a "silver lining" of sorts, she said, since "the closeness of death every day clarifies your perception and pulls away the things that aren't meaningful." The arts, it turns out, remain meaningful for those who have remained in Kharkiv during the horrors of 21st century warfare.

One of this summer's shows—*Orchestra*—looks to what comes next. Set in a small theater-café in postwar France, the audience becomes part of the setting. The proprietress, Madam Hortens, and her assistant Suzanne are bringing a women's orchestra to the stage. Both women, it turns out, are in love with the same man. The theater's showbill advertises a light, ironic comedy, or a "small mirror" on real life. As the play, full of heartbreaking surprises, continues, Kharkiv audiences see what they can look forward to once the present war ends: the minor sorrows of everyday life.

23: Kyiv Biennial Goes Pan-European

September 20, 2024

Kyiv Biennial 2023, the fifth edition of the show highlighting the newest Ukrainian and international art, went pan-European this year. Beginning in Kyiv in October, it cascaded across the continent, with a series of openings into 2024 in Kyiv, Ivano-Frankivsk, Uzhhorod, Berlin, Warsaw, Lublin, Antwerp, and Vienna.

The founders—Kyiv's Visual Culture Research Center with Austrian curators Hedwig Saxenhuber and Georg Schöllhammer—began the program as a response to the initial Russian seizure of Eastern Ukraine in 2014. Since 2015, the festival has offered an international forum for art, dialogue, and politics through interdisciplinary presentations of seminars, socially engaged visual art, and political activism. Previous iterations integrated contemporary Ukrainian and international artists and audiences into a single conversation as an introductory gesture to create bridges for long-term individual and institutional relationships, bringing Ukraine closer to the European arts community. Imagined as a grassroot, artist-led initiative, the biennial became a way for the Ukrainian art community to turn away from Russian ambition and look to the West.

This year's show explores the trauma unleashed by the Russian full-scale invasion of 2022. Its movable celebration brought together 120 artists, scholars, and activists to provide multiple perspectives on the displacement, decolonization, and psychological and ecological impacts of war. The organizers created an integrated program that was far more than just a biennial in exile.

The Berlin leg of the program series proved particularly noteworthy, in light of that city's place as arguably the most important center of contemporary art. Various art instillations, video sessions, seminars, lectures, and discussions spread out across the city at venues like the New Society for Visual Art, the Urban Culture Institute, Between Bridges, Prater Gallery, the Berlin outpost of the City Workshop based in Linz, Austria, and the Artspace Kreuzberg. Prominent and less-established artists from Germany and Ukraine

(Ukrainians both remaining in Ukraine as well as in exile across Europe) offered dozens of events, attracting Berlin's extensive arts community.

In addition to the various art exhibits, the Berlin shows included film screenings (such as *Chornobyl 22* by Oleksiy Radynski); lectures (by Timothy Snyder and others); panel discussions (with Kateryna Iakovlenko, Yassin al-Haj Saleh, and Jan Tomasz Gross, among others); and musical performances (such as Heinali's *Kyiv Eternal*). This wide range of offerings opened engagement between Ukrainian artists and their Berlin audiences.

Much of the Berlin programming between May and July focused on the question of time. What is the meaning of time at a moment when wars and instability of once secure political, social, and cultural regimes have brought the concept of sovereignty under attack? The art and accompanying discussions challenged peacetime notions of time with questions like: How different is the meaning of time during a military assault, occupation, displacement? How does our concept of time change when confronting a quagmire, a dead-end, a state of long-term suspended animation? How does the deprivation of a future-oriented imagination alter the sense of self? How does despair manifest itself? What is the meaning of "now" in the face of total uncertainty? Such queries were formulated and partially answered through artistic expression, which itself was disconnected from time.

None of the installations at any of the Biennial's Berlin stopover offer clear answers to such questions. But whatever the answers ultimately prove to be, this fifth Kyiv Biennial shows how they might be found through the artistic, intellectual, and cultural integration of Ukraine's vibrant artistic community with that of Europe.

24: "But I Am Happy"

September 27, 2024

Early this summer, Ukrainian pop songwriter and singer Klavdia Petrivna stopped to perform in the western Ukrainian city of Uzhhorod as part of a national tour. This concert was one among many for Petrivna, and for dozens of other Ukrainian pop stars during this third summer of war. Audiences around Ukraine embraced the momentary normality of hearing a favorite star, especially in Ukraine's far west, beyond easy reach of Russian attack. For a moment, the world could seem as it always had.

Petrivna, however, is not just another talented pop singer. Her mystique rests on her concealed identity, generating a guessing game as to who she really is. She shot to the center of Ukrainian youth culture quickly after coming onto the scene in 2023 thanks to massive popularity on TikTok, YouTube, and, ultimately, radio. Her crystalline voice, fresh lyrics about young love and mental health, bouncy pop rhythms, and innocence set just the right tone for those looking to escape the brutality and cynicism of war.

Petrivna has assumed the name of a character in Volodymyr Vinnychenko's 1917 carnivalesque classic *Notes of the Snub-nosed Mephistopheles*. The central character, a successful trickster lawyer named Yakov Mykhailiuk, is known to all by the character-defining nickname "Kirpaty Mephistopheles." On one level, the story revolves around a love triangle involving Sonya (the wife of former Communist Party official Dmytro Sosnytski), Sosnytski, and Mykhailiuk. Sonya can't figure out which one is the father of her baby Dmytro.

A parallel story focuses around Panas Pavlovich Kryvula, whom Mykhailiuk convinces should divorce his wife and go to another woman. Again, the messy realities of parenthood intervene.

Finally, Mykhailkiuk has a passing affair with Klavdia Petrivna, a single mother. Mykhailiuk moves on to another woman, who turns out to be his true love, only to have that relationship upended when Klavdia shows up with an unwanted son, Mika.

A renowned Ukrainian literary classic, the book is remembered for such lines as "The family cannot be destroyed from the outside. It always falls apart from the inside" and "It gives me pleasure to lure a man to the top of the mountain and push him down." The novel remains a classic tale of dysfunctional families upended by deceit.

The novel's import extends beyond its telling portrait of a society on the verge of revolutionary collapse. Vinnychenko, the writer of the story, was the first prime minister of the short-lived independent Ukrainian People's Republic. He traveled to Petrograd to plead Ukraine's cause just in time to witness the overthrow of the Russian Provisional Government by the Bolsheviks in 1917. He went abroad, only to return in 1920 to join the Bolsheviks in Moscow. Disappointed by what he saw as the Communists' "Great Russian chauvinism," he fled again to live in exile, first in Germany and then France. He was imprisoned by the Nazis for failing to collaborate with their regime. He died in exile in 1951.

The anonymous pop singer's selection of a character from a Vinnychenko work resonates with political as well as cultural significance. Vinnychenko's life in some ways represents a vision of a Ukrainian future for those fighting for their county's independence and integration into Europe. The connection to the character of Klavdia Petrivna speaks to the upheavals caused by the other woman.

Speculation over Klavdia's identity has run the gamut, from an 18-year-old music student from Lviv (Solomiya Opryshko); to well-known performer Masha Kondratenko (who appeared at a February 2024 awards ceremony to collect Petrivna's nomination for "Debut of the Year"); to an artificial intelligence anime character.

Fame has taken on a new meaning in the era of social media. Sometimes being mysterious captures more attention than becoming a familiar face. Identity guessing games may garner more fans than appearing as oneself (as the producers of the American TV series *The Masked Singer* can attest). This frisson expands during a period of war, when so much once thought to be known becomes uncertain; in this way, Petrivna's hidden identity is tailor-made for this moment in Ukraine.

25: Keep the Cameras Rolling

October 4, 2024

Rockets flew overhead as the Film.UA movie studio in Kyiv opened its large bomb shelters to neighborhood residents seeking protection during the first months of the Russian full-scale invasion. Many stayed for weeks, and one woman gave birth to a baby girl in a studio basement.

Founded in 2002 by lawyer Sergey Sozanovsky, Film.UA was, by 2022, one of the region's major production companies for new movies and television series. Sozanovsky had worked with Inter TV, where he hired a young comedian named Volodymyr Zelensky to star in a new television series, *Servant of the People*. He realized around his time that there was space within the Russian and Ukrainian media worlds for a studio company that could mount productions which were less expensive than importing films and shows from abroad.

Most of the new studio's business came from Russian television channels, but these orders disappeared in the wake of the 2014 Russian seizure of Crimea. The company turned further abroad in search of new markets. By 2022, it had released 14 feature films, several of which were sold to Netflix and European broadcasters. Orders for television miniseries from European stations began to roll in, as did work on documentary films from around the world.

After the February 2022 Russian invasion, Film.UA struggled to keep employees paid and neighbors safe. Many studio workers already had been working at home due to the COVID pandemic. Those who did not head off to the military wanted to help their country in any way possible. By mid-2022, production picked up, especially after the German distributor Red Arrow Studios International invested in a six-episode series about the war, *Those Who Stayed*. That series garnered top viewership on Netflix and various European streaming services and broadcast channels.

Recognizing that Ukrainian viewers had little interest in watching stories of a war unfolding outside their windows,

Film.UA turned to lighter fare for the domestic market. Box office sales in Ukraine for its full-length animated feature *Mavka: The Forest Song* have more than doubled the company's initial $8 million investment. Based on tales and characters drawn from Slavic mythology, this has been the company's most successful film to date, with spin-off products becoming staples of décor in Ukrainian children's bedrooms.

Ukrainian cinema has enjoyed artistic success for more than a century, with film studios in Odesa long forming a Eurasian Hollywood. Director Oleksandr Dovzhenko was one of the earliest Soviet master filmmakers, pioneering what would become Soviet montage theory. Sergei Parajanov, Sergei Bondarchuk, and Ihor Podolchak are but a few notable directors to emerge from Ukraine. Sozanovsky's wisdom lies in recognizing how he could leverage that legacy—and the scores of top professionals who made it possible—for 21st century success.

With eight sound stages, restaurants, shops, an outdoor village, botanical garden, and costume department, Film.UA's sprawling workshops are now a well-known presence in Kyiv's distant Troyeshchnya neighborhood. This area is, in many ways, indistinguishable from hundreds of other socialist neighborhoods built in the 1960s, 1970s, and 1980s anywhere between Berlin and Beijing. Few physical indicators suggest a Ukrainian Hollywood in the making.

Shortly after independence, however, one of the Ukrainian capital's most robust, if scraggly, markets grew up here. As authorities cracked down on small-scale merchants in the city's center, they gathered along open fields straddling the city's northeast border. This spatial ambiguity between jurisdictions lent some security from official harassment (although criminal gangs known in Ukraine as "mafias" quickly moved into this power vacuum).

The market attracted large numbers of immigrant merchants and their families, and by the beginning of this century, Troyeshchnya had become home to significant Afghan, Vietnamese, Pakistani, Indian, and Chinese communities. The market grew to more than 5,000 stalls at its height, employing some 20,000 Kyivans, making the neighborhood one of the city's most dynamic by the time Film.UA set up shop. Home to nearly a quarter-million residents before 2022, the area's post-independence social and economic vitality made it a suitable spot for a film studio.

The war has further cemented the relationship between studio and city. Film.UA's continuing success despite the ongoing war, combined with Troyeshchnya's vitality, point to a possible postwar future that can sustain Ukraine through difficult times.

26: A World Where Russia Is Past and Ukraine Is Future

October 11, 2024

War frequently leads people to imagine what will come once peace arrives. How can we visualize what will follow? How can we think about making that envisioned future real? Such questions run through art created at a time of war, even as such creativity focuses on the human catastrophe that war generates. This juxtaposition of horror and disgust for the reality of the present with the hope that all will be better once the fighting ends commands a leap of imagination.

Kyiv Modern-Ballet Theater's inspirational choreographer Radu Poklitar has observed that he creates his own world because he can't do anything else. The worlds he and his company build on the stage help them and their audiences confront the devastation of war and dream of a future that will arrive with peace. The Moldova-born, Moscow- and Odesa-trained Poklitar and his company have steadfastly performed throughout the war. They have drawn on their commitment to expressive modern dance in order to explore some of the most emotional challenges confronting war-torn Ukraine.

An evening of two one-act ballets in May explicitly explored the necessity of Ukrainians deciding for themselves the future they want to embrace. Both works served as allegories about the values of democratic society.

The program began with *Discrimination*, a new work set to the music of George Frideric Handel and contemporary Ukrainian composer Valentyn Sylvestrov. The ballet presents a series of parables depicting various forms of discrimination. The seemingly nonlinear piece slowly reveals the emotions that lead to disagreement and prejudice. Expressions of tolerance and mutual understanding performed through dance ultimately reveal the values of a democratic society that rise above difference. The choreography's continuous movements amplify the preeminence of democratic values for the Ukrainian future.

Poklitar set *Tomorrow*, the evening's second work, to the music of Frédéric Chopin. Performed on a bare, semi-lit stage, the dancers perform in costumes casting the colors of flickering flames, representing the divine energy within every human being. Kinetic physicality tells stories of quotidian travails. Chopin's music creates an ethereal harmony that contrasts with the rhythms of modern life. Present-day troubles diminish in significance as dance turns to a future in which such concerns no longer matter. As one reviewer noted after the work's March 2023 premier, this is a show emphasizing that Russia is the past and Ukraine is the future.

Staged at the October Palace, the performance's venue has its own history of joys and horrors. Architect Vikentiy Beretti designed the neoclassical palace as the Kyiv Institute for Noble Maidens during the 1830s and 1840s. The Soviet Cheka (predecessor to the KGB) claimed the building as its headquarters following the Bolshevik revolution. Cheka officers killed about 120,000 in the building before it was destroyed by German bombs during World War II. Renovated during the 1950s as a concert hall, the building has been an important performance setting ever since. Its history symbolizes fate's twists and turns, especially in Ukraine and Kyiv.

Poklitar envisions the Kyiv Modern-Dance Theater as a creative space for movement that offers bold experimentation together with original readings of world-famous ballets. Over the course of the war, he has fostered a laboratory on stage, one that empowers his audiences to consider what their—and Ukraine's—future might be. The imaginary worlds he and his company create through dance enable futures that are Ukrainian, no matter how Russian they may have been in the past.

27: Music Full of Light

October 18, 2024

Odesan evenings in June can be stunning in peacetime, as the scent of generous flowering trees and plants unfolds over a city luxuriating in soft evening breezes off the Black Sea. A vibrant beach scene transforms, as hedonistic nighttime clubbers replace daytime sun worshippers. Understanding why so many who have passed through the city proclaim it to be extraordinary requires little imagination.

This past June, alas, was not a time of peace.

The Odesa Philharmonic, led by Hobart Earle, traditionally closes its season with a rousing celebration. But the orchestra's final concert this year, performed on the evening of June 14, almost didn't take place, as air raid sirens sounded and the electricity went off just as the orchestra was warming up during a last-minute rehearsal. The orchestra scrambled to use temporary generators to cast some light on their music stands. Maestro Earle wondered how he could conduct a Brahms symphony in the dark. The phrase of the hour was "stay flexible," which is how Ukrainians keep going despite the travails that have beset them since the Russian full-scale invasion.

Once the all clear sounded, the lights came back on, and audience members had taken their seats, the orchestra began with the premier of a haunting new work, Evgeni Orkin's *Elegy* (Op. 90). Orkin composed the piece in memory of the Odesa victims of the current war. This somber, moving, and, at times, disturbing eight-minute reflection on the horror of loss in wartime begins with a momentary crash of cymbals before moving to a quietly sorrowful meditation on war's assault on the lyricism of peace. The orchestra and audience stood in silence at the end.

Orkin's piece set a somber mood in a distinctly modern style. His life and career track with those of many other top Ukrainian musicians of his generation. Born in Lviv in 1977, he studied clarinet and composition at the Kyiv Conservatory before seeking further training in the Netherlands. He kept a foothold in the Ukrainian classical music scene, even as he pursued opportunities in Europe. He played as principal clarinet in the Kyiv Camerata ensemble during the early 1990s, while simultaneously co-founding the Open-Lift project promoting contemporary music in Utrecht.

Orkin began composing chamber symphonies; symphonies; concertos for violin, piano, saxophone, and clarinet; and operas. His chamber opera, *The Fairy Tale of the Forest Kings* (*Das Märchen der Waldkönigin Ach*), brought a Ukrainian fairytale to the stage at the Staatstheater Wiesbaden in 2023, while his *Odessa Rhapsody* earned him the European Music Prize, awarded by the mayor of Berlin. This June, his *Todesfuge*, inspired by Paul Celan's poem about the Nazi genocide of the Jews, premiered at the Vienna Festival. This background helps to explain how the Odesa concert came together.

The concert closed with a luxurious performance of Johannes Brahms's Symphony No. 2 in D major, op. 73. Brahms composed this pastoral work during a summer sojourn in the Austrian town of Pörtschach am Wörthersee. Now much beloved, Brahms warned his publisher that he had "never written anything so sad, and the score must come out in mourning." Concertgoers ever since have admired the gripping beauty found in the composer's self-proclaimed sense of melancholy. In the hands of Earle and his orchestra, the piece captured both the sorrow of this moment and the bucolic beauty of the exceptional city they call home.

During the lead-up to the performance, the orchestra's website urged people to consider attending this concert, saying that Brahms's symphony "is full of light, gentle melodies. You will definitely like it and it will put you in a great mood [with] an incredible charge of energy," since the score would be like "musical medicine, which is so necessary for all Ukrainians." An additional benefit: the audience "will be able to listen to the world premiere of a Ukrainian composer and be at the center of the musical life of Ukraine." When Maestro Earle lowered his baton that evening (and on the orchestra's season), it was before an audience steeped in both melancholy and beauty.

28: Nothing Stops a Kyiv Puppet

October 25, 2024

The close of Kyiv's Academic Puppet Theater's 97th season in June was a moment of frustration and pride. Russian bombardment of the city, leading to extensive blackouts, had frustrated the theater's efforts to bring one more premiere performance to audiences before summer. Theater management struggled with finding alternative power sources that would allow operations to continue without access to the city grid, even while new productions moved forward throughout the season. But the company took great pride in what it had been able to accomplish over the difficult autumn-to-spring term. Despite wartime hardships, it staged 273 performances, including four premiers, before more than 50,000 spectators of all ages.

Actors Vadym Dotsenko, Yury Farafonov, and Oleksandr Voron appeared in more than 177 performances each, carrying the company along throughout this difficult period. Newcomers joined these veterans to guarantee artistic and commercial success. As a result of these efforts, the company was among the most profitable among all Ukrainian theaters.

Beyond what was happening on stage, the theater held master classes with other cultural centers, joined with the State Toy Museum to mount a large exhibit of dolls, and hosted colleagues from Kherson and Mykolaiv. Charitable activities included visits to theaters and children's libraries, as well as special performances for military children, displaced persons, and adults and children with disabilities. In June, the company performed *The Cat and the Rooster* in sign language, with plans for creating more works for the hearing impaired.

Among these accomplishments—and despite constant interruption from Russian rockets—the company staged four premiers. Mykola Danko's stylish, fresh take on the Hans Christian Anderson classic *Thumbelina* joined longtime favorites such as *The Golden Chicken* and the Ukrainian tale *Ivasik-Telesic* to delight younger viewers. A new, large-scale musical production of *The Wizard of Oz* drew older audiences.

In addition, a New Year's holiday medley, *Bloggers in the Theater*, entered the company's regular repertoire. The play highlights the puppet world as a magical place as three bloggers sneak into the theater at night to shoot stories for their Instagram and TikTok accounts. Their steps and missteps cast light on the vanishing line between fantasy and reality that has stood at the center of fairy tales for centuries and is the fulcrum of social media today.

A late-season extravaganza, *Stolen Happiness*, based on Ivan Franko's popular play, explores difficult choices between freedom and security. Star performer Dmytro Linartovych took time from his military service to play gendarme Mykhailo Hurman in this story of unhappy love. Director Tetyana Avramenko presents the well-known story as a contemporary tragedy of characters robbed of their futures, where one set of choices will betray others. Only by accepting the irreversibility of life's circumstances can we face the future with courage. For Avramenko, the story reveals pain that is felt in the protagonists' souls, and in the souls of the show's wartime audiences.

Looking back at its 97th season, company members at Kyiv's Academic Puppet Theater find plenty of reasons to celebrate. Rather than focusing on blackouts, shortened performance times, restricted audience size, and physical damage from nearby attacks, the company chooses to look to its future, approaching its 98th season with a combination of optimism and defiance. In doing so, it personifies characteristics that have marked Kyiv's—and Ukraine's—cultural life from the very first days of the Russian full-scale invasion.

29: Ruslana's Defiance in the Face of Horror

November 1, 2024

Within hours of the massive Russian missile attack on Kyiv's children's hospital on July 8, Ukrainian rock star Ruslana took to Instagram to denounce what she decried as an act of terrorism carried out with the highest degree of cynicism. The daylight attacks on the Okhmatdyt Hospital, Ukraine's largest and, by reputation, best children's hospital, accompanied a barrage of Russian raids unleashed across Ukraine, killing at least 41 Ukrainians. These attacks came as NATO leaders gathered in Washington to celebrate the alliance's 75th anniversary. Rather than disheartening Ukrainians into submission, however, Russia has provoked greater anger and disgust.

Ruslana's outrage was more than performative. Known for her activism against judicial arbitrariness, environmental degradation, and human trafficking (she was a UNICEF Goodwill Ambassador in 2004 and 2005), the fate of Ukraine's children has long been at the center of her activism. Following her 2004 Eurovision Song Contest victory, she organized a charity concert for children suffering from the consequences of the Chernobyl nuclear power plant accident. Soon thereafter, she joined with German rock star Peter Maffay on a monthlong German tour to gather funds to benefit children in need. She has frequently performed in charity concerts for children's hospitals in Kyiv, Lviv, and Dnipro. Singer, songwriter, dancer, actor, activist, and former politicians, she has drawn on her international renown to advance various social and political causes.

Ruslana Stepanivna Lyzhychko grew up in the Lviv region during the late 1970s and 1980s, the daughter of a Ukrainian father and a Russian mother. Her mother encouraged her musical talents, as did the popular singer Vasyl Zinkevuch. She studied at the Lviv Conservatory in the early 1990s with prominent Ukrainian composers and conductors such as Mykola Kolessa. "Wild Dances," her Eurovision-winning song, has become a pop classic with worldwide recognition. She served for a time in the Verkhovna Rada, the

Ukrainian parliament; made the 2013 *Forbes* list of the most influential women in the world; and received the US Secretary of State's International Women of Courage Award in 2014. The Spanish newspaper *El Mundo* has compared her to Joan of Arc.

Her voice, be it lifted in song or spoken in anger, carries weight. Ruslana's cries that July day were seen as especially heartfelt in light of her long support for children's medical research and care. Over the weeks that followed, there was an outpouring of revulsion by Ukrainians in Ukraine and around the world.

In a fundraising appeal on her official Facebook page on July 8, Ruslana urged Ukrainians to turn their rage into justified revenge.

"When you read the news about being hit by the children's hospital, where at that time the planned operations for the smallest patients were conducted... when you read that there [could] be children under the rubble, you can no longer control pain or rage," she wrote. She urged her compatriots to turn that rage into revenge and "kick the enemy out of our land."

The attacks on July 8 were but a portion of the destruction let loose on Ukraine by Russian rocket assaults this summer. As Russia has demonstrated repeatedly in Ukraine, Syria, and elsewhere, it has tremendous power to destroy. Ukraine, on the other hand, as demonstrated by the response to the hospital bombing, repeatedly reveals a capacity for renewal in the face of unfathomable suffering. Ruslana personifies the country's defiance in the face of horror. She is not alone.

30: London's Finborough Theatre Shines Light on Mariupol

November 8, 2024

Few Britons or Americans had ever heard of Mariupol before 2022. The southern Ukrainian steel town and port of around 120,000 residents did not attract many tourists. But now, more than two and a half years after the Russian full-scale invasion, the occupied rust-belt city has become a symbol of Russian brutality, thanks to news coverage of the three-month Russian siege in 2022, and Stystav Chernov's documentary about it, *20 Days in Mariupol*. The film won the 2024 Oscar for best documentary feature. A few months later, Inna Goncharova's powerful play about the city, *The Trumpeter*, won critical acclaim at its premiere at London's Finborough Theatre in July.

Goncharova's script tells the true story of the lone survivor of one of Ukraine's marine brigade bands at Mariupol, a trumpeter trapped for 80 days with other Ukrainian fighters in the underground labyrinth under the massive Azovstal steel plant. Held up with companions by an unrelenting Russian artillery barrage, the trumpeter desperately tries to find harmony in his music as he plans to compose a "symphony of war."

The small theater is blacked out, with just four chairs on stage. The trumpeter is joined by three other characters sheltering in the same bunker. The audience learns about the trumpeter's life as a musician against the constant backdrop of shaking walls and falling ceilings. Russian bombs interrupt his efforts to understand why he has failed as a composer. His constant self-reflection and horn tooting increasingly irritate his bunker mates, whose nerves are frayed from living through constant attack. The play becomes a 60-minute search for harmony amid cacophony.

Playwright Goncharova is a writer, actor, director, and public figure in the Kyiv theater community. She teamed up with admired actor Peter Mironov in 2022 to bring this play to Kyiv audiences.

English writer John Farndon included the work among several wartime Ukrainian plays he translated for the London stage. *The Guardian's* David Jays found *The Trumpet* to provide a feverish foray into the mind of warriors through a work that pays passionate homage to Ukraine's lost musicians.

Veteran London actor Kristin Milwad dominates the production as the trumpeter, as did Mironov in Kyiv. Jays reports that Milwad "rattles with vitality, stretching an incongruous smile despite the circumstances." He writes, "We don't hear the composer's music but Milwad performs a vocal symphony: smoke-voiced anxiety, bellows of bombardment, a voice worn to wisp by fear—and the rasp of breath in the darkness that means survival."

A renowned showcase for new theater, the diminutive Finborough has worked closely with Farndon and the Worldwide Ukrainian Play Readings project to bring Ukrainian works to London. Their collaborations include a highly praised production of Neda Nejdana's *Pussycat in Memory of Darkness*, also featuring Milwad.

As audiences of this summer's Finborough plays and last winter's documentary film discovered, Mariupol's anguish encapsulates the tragedy of the current war in Ukraine. A Ukrainian Everytown, the city's ordinariness speaks to the torment Ukrainians face about their past failures and future potential, as well as to the hopes and fears of anyone anywhere during wartime.

31: Seeking a Wider View of What Constitutes Ukrainian Art

November 15, 2024

Ukraine's shifting 20th-century borders complicate the meaning of ideas like "Ukrainian art" and "Ukrainian culture." Many groups have lived on the territory of today's Ukraine and many territories of Ukraine have been included within the borders of different political states. This is particularly true of Lviv, where Poles, Jews, Armenians, Austrians, as well as Ukrainians, have long added to the local culture. Art historian, writer, and poet Bohdana Pinchevska dives into the center of these varied contributions in her book *Art by Jewish Artists of Galicia in the Years 1900–1939* which, though published in 2013, is getting a new look in light of the current war.

Pinchevska's groundbreaking work began with her dissertation for the National Academy of Fine Arts and Architecture in Kyiv. The academy required graduate students to write dissertations examining topics related to some aspect of the arts located in Ukraine. Firm in her decision not to explore anything from the Soviet period, she began to look for topics connected to pre-Soviet art or art from locations not incorporated into the Soviet Union at the time. She also wanted a topic outside the mainstream that would be of interest to her.

These constraints led her to Galicia and Lviv early in the 20th century, and to the fascinating story of secular Jewish artists who emerged there. This school of art flourished from 1900 until 1939, when it collapsed during the Holocaust, leaving few traces.

Pinchevska begins her story with the Jewish sector at a European industrial and art exhibition in Paris in 1900. Artists from around Europe brought together decorative, applied, and sacred art depicting Jewish life. The Kraków School of Fine Arts, the leading art institution in Galicia, had already become one of the few educational institutions in the region to admit Jewish students after oil prince Maurycy Gottlieb showed up to study with Jan Matejko. The talented Gottlieb impressed Matejko, who committed himself to the open enrollment of Jewish students following Gottlieb's untimely death.

Matejko encouraged a vision of national art depicting key moments in history. Gottlieb, his favorite student, embraced this notion and eventually emerged as the father of Jewish secular art. While much has been written about Gottlieb, there was no monograph examining his connections to Ukraine when Pinchevska began her research, even though he was born in Drohobych.

Pinchevska set out to fill this scholarly lacuna. She settled on students at the Kraków School who had entered "Judaism" under "Religion" in their applications but pursued art that was secular and connected with the rising modernism of the period. Their integration into the European and national art worlds led some to question whether there even was such a thing as a distinctive Jewish secular art.

Pinchevska argues that two general schools of secular Jewish art emerged: a Ukrainian community revolving around the Gottlieb family and a Polish line focused on Samuel Hirszenberg, the distinguished painter of Jewish life. Jewish artists studied together and hung out together in Kraków, Warsaw, Paris, and, eventually, Lviv.

They often brought significant collections of Jewish art with them when they returned to Lviv, where the Lviv Polytechnic Institute became a center of debate around what made Jewish art Jewish. This lively scene continued into the interwar period, only to be destroyed by the arrival of the Soviets, and then the Nazis, and the unleashing of the Holocaust in 1939.

Pinchevska and other art historians and cultural critics coming of age following Ukrainian independence have provided an important foundation for exploring the nature of Ukrainian art that transcends the confines of ethnic boundaries. She makes a compelling case that it is not possible to understand Lviv's cultural heritage without incorporating all the artistic strands that have come together in the city. The same holds for Galicia and for Ukraine more generally. What might have remained an obscure doctoral dissertation on a buried topic has taken on broad significance and now stands at the center of a national debate over what Ukrainian culture is and is not.

32: Reclaiming Ukrainian Cultural Heroes from the Soviet Era

November 22, 2024

The venerable Cleveland Orchestra invited Ukrainian conductor Oksana Lyniv to lead one of its Blossom Music Center concerts this summer. Lyniv, who was the first female music director of an Italian opera house (the Teatro Comunale di Bologna) and the first woman to conduct at Bayreuth, has promoted Ukrainian classical music tirelessly as she has become a leading candidate for several music director positions with major orchestras around the world.

Her July appearance in Cleveland featured Leoš Janáčk's *Cunning Little Vixen Suite,* Sergei Rachmaninov's *Rhapsody on a Theme of Paganini,* Igor Stravinsky's *The Firebird Suite,* and Boris Lyatoshynsky's *Grazhya Symphonic Ballad.* Lyniv's presentation of Lyatoshynsky's work won particular praise. Writing for the website Bachtrack, critic Frank Kuznik found this performance "a gripping narrative, colorful and exciting, bristling with the sounds of battle." He continued, "For a visiting conductor to achieve that level of detail and visual quality in a one-off with the orchestra was truly remarkable."

Lyniv's previous accomplishments enabled her to feature Lyatoshynsky's once obscure music. The composer's works were largely unknown in the West before the current war prompted performances across Europe and North America. The Cleveland concert is but one of several bringing Ukrainian classical music—including that of Lyatoshynsky—into the mainstream symphonic repertoire worldwide.

Lyatoshynsky's Soviet musical legacy poses challenges for reconstituting a Ukrainian musical tradition. Widely recognized as a leading member of the founding generation of 20th century Ukrainian composers, Lyatoshynsky was born in Zhytomyr in 1895 into a household steeped in Polish literature and history. He entered Kyiv University's School of Law in 1913 before being employed to teach at the Kyiv Conservatory. He composed music in several genres throughout the 1910s. He entered the Soviet musical mainstream, studying folk music and composing folk ballets in Tajikistan during the 1930s and joined the faculty of the Moscow Conservatory. He composed two operas, *The Golden Ring* and *Shchors*, during this period.

Lyatoshynsky began arranging Ukrainian songs while the Kyiv Conservatory was in wartime exile in Saratov. He simultaneously worked to save Ukrainian musical manuscripts from destruction at the hands of the Nazis.

Following the war, he turned to composing symphonic works (including five symphonies, the *Grazhyna*, as well as his *Taras Shevchenko* and *Romeo and Juliet* suites, and a "Slavic" piano concerto). Soviet authorities banned some of his compositions, such as his Second Symphony, during the restrictive Stalinist years following World War II. Despite flirtations with what Stalinist critics considered to be "formalism," Lyatoshynsky received top accolades from the Soviet regime, including two Stalin Prizes.

Lyatoshynsky was named People's Artist of the Ukrainian SSR the year of his death, 1968. He had become recognized by this time as one of the important promoters of modernism in Ukrainian classical music through his compositions and his teaching. Several of his students became leaders in the Kyiv avant-garde movement of the 1960s and 1970s. His efforts to integrate Ukrainian and Polish musical motifs into a 20th century European classical repertoire increasingly won praise from promoters of Ukrainian culture, despite his complex relationship with the Soviet government.

In January 2022, the Kyiv Symphony Orchestra established the Lyatoshynsky Club as a "community of passionate people from culture and business, aimed at discovering, multiplying and promoting Ukrainian music at home and abroad." The club views its establishment as an effort to represent Ukrainian national art, "a large part of which remained unknown to the public due to the ideological vices of colonial policy."

Lyatoshynsky was a Soviet composer whose compositions, teaching, and preservation efforts helped a Ukrainian classical music canon to emerge. He represents numerous cultural figures who built careers during the Soviet period and nurtured the conditions for a modern, post-Soviet Ukrainian culture to coalesce following independence. His music demonstrates the ways in which identifying creative artists as "Soviet" obscures as much of their legacies as it clarifies.

This summer's concert in Ohio placed Lyatoshynsky's symphonic work among other well-known "Slavic" composers such as Janáčk, Rachmaninov, and Stravinsky. Such attention—especially at the masterful hands of conductor Lyniv and one of the world's top symphonies, the Cleveland Orchestra—opens ears to a Ukrainian classical tradition hidden for too long behind labels like *Soviet* and *European*.

33: A Real-Life Titus Andronicus in Eastern Ukraine

November 27, 2024

"The play *Titus Andronicus* is considered the worst thing Shakespeare ever wrote. It's so bad there's doubt as to whether *they* even wrote it. There's too much meaningless evil in the play, and almost no logic.... But no.... It's not overdone at all. The play *Titus Andronicus* is being performed on the stages of Slovyansk, Kramatorsk, Donetsk, Horlivka, Luhansk... Hieronymus Bosch is doing the stage scenery." Diarist Olena Stiazhkina wrote these words over the weekend of May 16–17, 2014, as she tried to make sense of what was transpiring all around her in eastern Ukraine.

A history professor in her hometown Donetsk, Stiazhkina published fiction on the side in her native Russian prior to the war, often using the pen name Olena Iurska. Looking back, she feels guilt at having enjoyed considerable success and garnered several prizes as a Russian author. All of this changed on March 2, 2014, when "little green men" dispatched from the Russian Federation linked up with pro-Russian forces in Donetsk and Luhansk to bring down Ukrainian rule.

The professional historian in Stiazhkina prompted her to start a diary, which begins on March 2 and ends on August 18, 2014, recording the chaos, horror, and inhumanity unfolding around her. Her wartime journal became available in June in English translation as *Ukraine, War, Love: A Donetsk Diary* through the Harvard Library of Ukrainian Literature.

Russian President Vladimir Putin understood that an invasion without an invasion—dispatching troops who were not wearing clear identification in 2014—allowed politicians in the West to look the other way. Even more cynically, they looked away even after so-called separatist forces brought down a civilian Malaysian Airways flight on its way from Amsterdam to Kuala Lumpur a few months later. She and her compatriots understood that a war had begun with Russia.

Prior to 2014, Stiazhkina wasn't clear precisely who she was. Like many of us, she claimed many identities: historian, writer, mother, university professor, grateful reader, friend, wife, daughter. The order among these distinctions didn't really matter; context did. After March 2014, one identity, she wrote, was "permanently in first place now. I'm a Ukrainian."

On May 11, she set out a sarcastic methodological handbook for the new invaders. "You can print out ballots on any printer. No need to be delicate here. You can have a lot of ballots. Or not. The quantity is not important. Later, you'll count them as instructed anyway. If you need more, add some. If you've got too many, toss some.... Don't use numbers over one hundred. Be aware that certain people don't believe that something can win a hundred and fifteen percent of the votes. Well, right now they don't. But we'll fix that."

Titus Andronicus-level horror runs throughout her diary, as it does through Shakespeare's ultimate revenge play, with too many examples to record here. Perhaps one scene will suffice: "We are polite people," she observes. "Other 'polite people'—with strong accents from the Caucasus—killed three men. First, they tortured them. They opened their bellies. The victims were still alive.... And they were still alive when they were thrown into the river.... That's Slovyansk. That's the 'Russian world.'"

As a historian, she ponders what the conflict will mean when historians of a future era look back. "Later we will give this war a name," she decides. "Our day of victory will be this war's end. But this war's beginning was in March 2014."

She stops recording events in August 2014, as she begins a new life in Kyiv and at universities around Europe and the United States. She does so by observing, "All war diaries are histories of suffering. Anne Frank, Tanya Savicheva.... 'Everyone is dead.'" She continues, "But you know something? All my people are alive. Lotya and Surikova, and the photographer, and Granny Shura, and even Astro the poodle. We're alive. Heroes don't die." And neither does Ukraine.

34: Celebrating Films that Touch Souls

December 6, 2024

The story of the making of Dmytro Moiseev's feature film *Grey Bees* is worthy of a film in and of itself. Moiseev and his team were in full production in Severodonetsk when Russia launched its full-scale invasion in 2022. That city, located in the Luhansk region, would fall into Russian hands in heavy fighting within months. Somehow, the filmmakers were able to keep going, elsewhere, until they completed the film a year later.

Moiseev based his film on illustrious Ukrainian writer Andrey Kurkov's tender 2018 novel of the same name, about a beekeeper and a neighbor who choose to remain in the grey zone between armies to protect their bees. The book garnered critical acclaim in Ukraine and abroad, with Boris Dralyuk's translation winning the 2022 American National Book Critics Circle Award for translated fiction.

After gaining critical acclaim abroad, Moiseev's film won the Golden Duke award for the best new Ukrainian feature film at this year's Odesa International Film Festival, Ukraine's largest and most important film fest. Over the course of the past decade and a half, the festival has become known for the most anticipated premiers of Ukrainian films, the debut of young talents, and an opportunity to catch films for the first time. The award statues are a miniature version of Odesa's famous statue of the city's founder, the Duc de Richelieu.

This year, the festival was held in Kyiv due to security considerations. Film actor Daria Tregubova and television personality Vadum Karpyak presided over the opening and closing ceremonies. In between, the sold-out festival offered 15 programs and retrospectives, 92 screenings (including 56 Ukrainian films), and more than 40 industry-related events. There was a section for films generated by artificial intelligence. Special honors were given to those moviemaking heroes who have died defending Ukraine against Russian aggression.

Festival president Victoria Tigipko thanked the Ukrainian filmmakers and film buffs who have managed to keep the art form alive under the most difficult conditions. A number of Ukrainian sponsors—including the Ukrainian Cultural Fund, Kyivstar, and ICTV2—found the resources to keep going, helped along by several international partners, including Mazda, *Harper's Bazaar*, the Polish Institute, and Radisson Blu hotels. German Films brought several important movies, including Sara Summa's *Arthur & Diana*, Benjamin Plohl's *Jupiter*, and a German-Georgian joint production, *Gondola*.

The festival jury named Ksenia Kravtsova's *Glyadyelov* the best documentary film. Kravtsova's documentary celebrates the famous Ukrainian photographer Oleksandr Glyadyelov. The camera crew traveled around the country with Glyadyelov, including to Odesa, where he meets the founder of the Bright House shelter, Father Oleksandr Chumakov. In Bucha, he is present at the exhumation of bodies after the expulsion of the Russian army. A bit later, Glyadyelov is shown in Transcarpathia together with eco-activists who clear rivers, forests, and lawns of garbage. The result is a stunning portrayal of life in today's Ukraine.

Another entry, Serhyi Masloboyshchikov's new movie, *Yasa*, brings together two memorable women linked by Ukraine's decades-long civil unrest and war. Darka, a 20-something with multiple burn spots on her face, is being examined by cosmetologists at a Kyiv clinic. Hanna, an imposing woman in her 50s, is chatting on the phone nearby as their story slowly unfolds. The tale began when a man was killed during Kyiv's Euromaidan uprising in 2014. That man—the son of the older woman and the boyfriend of the younger woman—emerges as the central point of conflict and division between the two characters. Hanna blames Darka for the death of her son, saying that she was the one who drew him to the Maidan. Earlier, his mother had sent him to study and live peacefully in America. Instead, he died in the civil unrest unfolding in central Kyiv. The two women would next see one another a year later, when Hanna took Darka, a volunteer in the Russian-Ukrainian war who had been wounded in the fighting for control of Donetsk, from the field hospital to help her recover. Masloboyshchikov uses their relationship to expose the divisions and trauma Ukrainians have faced over the past decade.

British film director, screenwriter, and composer Michael Figgis caught this year's festival's significance when he told the audience, "I agree with the thesis that cinema can be a weapon. But it can also be medicine. And it is precisely in this role that cinematography has gathered significance in the 21st century—it has become something that serves human souls."

Film—indeed, all art forms—continues to feed Ukrainian souls, which explains in part why so many Ukrainians are seeking out films, theater performances, music, and literature during this time of existential threat. This year's Odesa International Film Festival fed many souls over its nine-day run.

Moiseev's film, and the Kurkov novel on which it is based, point to the pain suffered by too many Ukrainians. In responding to a Western journalist's questions about *Grey Bees*, Kurkov pondered the importance to Ukrainians of the concept of "home." What is "home," he asked, "when a foreign enemy has destroyed your neighborhood, your garden, and your feeling of safety?"

A film festival at a time of war is far more than an enjoyable time. This year's Odesa film celebration in Kyiv touches the souls of Ukrainians seeking an understanding of the world as it gets reshaped before their eyes.

35: Building a Thriving Ukrainian Design Community Now

December 13, 2024

Ukraine's diverse and often fragmented design community gathered in Kyiv over a late summer weekend in August. For the second year in a row, DVRZ Design Days offered a program of expositions, interactive zones, lectures, and workshops at four sites spread across the Ukrainian capital, from the Sviatoshyn District in the west to Podil and Kurenivka to the north.

Ukraine's interior, urban, industrial, fashion, graphic, and civil designers have not thought of themselves as a single profession. Some of these divisions are characteristic of an occupation that often divides itself between those who lean towards artistic pursuits and those who are drawn towards commerce and engineering. Soviet tendencies to box off professions by categories only intensified such differences.

Faced with the collapse of a state-dominated centralized economy following independence, many design fields fell prey to rapacious privateers. As Design Days organizer Larisa Tsybina put it, "even before the war, the development of Ukrainian design was very fragmented and slow. We did not have support from the state, from foundations that could take care of this area."

Other divisions emerged as well, between those looking to push Ukrainian design towards contemporary trends in Europe and those who cherish more traditional approaches to the visual environment. Some trendsetters sought to integrate old and new, as well as Western and Ukrainian design, with varying degrees of success. Until now, they often have cut off those looking back and those looking forward.

Design in all of its divisions will be at the center of any attempt to rebuild Ukraine following the current war. Postwar Ukraine will require freshly designed engineering infrastructure, new symbolic visions for a distinctly Ukrainian look in fashion and iconography, fresh architectural approaches to cityscapes, and technical standards which are in sync with those of Europe. At present, divisions in the design world—which range from the profession's various subfields to various ideological perspectives on the appropriate balance between the national and international—put a unified approach to the country's postwar reconstruction in question.

Tsybina and her colleagues have organized the Design Days event to begin the process of bridging the gaps between areas of the design profession, of attracting students to consider careers in the design field, and of educating the public about why design is important. They hope that such collaboration will make it possible to work with Ukrainian materials to design boldly and to address the challenges ahead. The Design Days gatherings also seek to find new ways to bring the achievements of Ukrainian designers to the international community.

These goals are present as well in a new magazine focusing on Ukrainian design, launched in May. According to its editors, *The Chronicle of Ukrainian Design* "is an attempt to see and show how Ukrainian design identity was born and evolved." The editors and sponsors are looking to rediscover a distinctive design history that reveals what was lost during the Soviet era. The magazine covers all areas of design in an effort to present a holistic vision that is functional, respectful of tradition, and innovative.

Magazine co-founder Nastichka Zherebetska described the mission this way on the website: "Ukrainian culture is on the verge of annihilation again, so we need to invest as much as possible in preserving the existing and restoring the forgotten. We need to find ourselves, dig into history, fill in historical gaps and talk about what Ukrainian design is. And for a modern designer, this is almost the only opportunity to somehow make a mark in this fast-paced world."

Ukraine's ability to rebuild following the war rests in part on the capacity of its professional design community to enable physical, symbolic, and spiritual reconstruction. The establishment of the DVRZ Design Days and the launching of *The Chronicle of Ukrainian Design* both recognize that such success will rest on developing the professional, artistic, and intellectual prerequisites for a thriving design community now.

36: A Circus Brings Joy to Lviv's Children

December 20, 2024

No place in Ukraine has been immune from the suffering of war over the past two and a half years. But even as men and women from across Ukraine have been fighting at the front and as their children have been exposed to constant trauma, uncertainty, and loss, military and civilian authorities, joined with various performing arts organizations, have tried to create pockets of tranquility so that children might forget about living through a time of war, even briefly.

Special performances by the Lviv State Circus this past spring and summer have been among those efforts to protect childhood wonder. Partnering with the Lviv Regional Military Administration and the charity My Dad Protects Ukraine, the circus staged special performances for more than 1,500 children from across the Lviv region, a relatively peaceful area in western Ukraine. These audiences included many whose parents are fighting in eastern Ukraine. As Lviv Military District Deputy Chief Hrystyna Zamulka put it in a quote on the Moryshn Rayon website, "Childhood should be happy. Unfortunately, our enemy is trying to take it away from Ukrainian children. Today we are able to be at this performance thanks to our defenders, thanks to your parents."

Housed in a concrete domed arena typical of Soviet-era circus buildings from the 1960s, the Lviv company remained part of a provincial circus circuit which fed to ever higher-ranking companies in union republic capitals such as Kyiv, and then on to Leningrad and Moscow. This regional status, however, never diminished the joy the company brought to children throughout the city and region.

All Ukrainian circuses struggled following independence, as did many performing arts institutions throughout the country. The Lviv company added an ice show and a water circus to attract new audiences. Director Roman Zdrenyk told journalist Kulkeba Alina last December that no circus in Ukraine has been able to mount large-scale acts for some time. Some of the country's leading performers head abroad and do not return. He complained about a shortage of clowns.

Such deficiencies, he argued, have made Ukrainian circuses more innovative as they try to meet audience demands with fewer resources. Circus managers have come to rely on younger performers and new technologies such as laser shows to enchant viewers. The current war has amplified these trends.

Lviv's Hapsburgian history has shaped the local circus. Aquatic acts in Lviv can trace their development back to the city's Sidoli Circus, which brought performers from Vienna to perform in water tanks as early as 1891. Cinema sessions—a distant precursor to today's video and laser shows—arrived at Lviv circuses from the imperial heartland in 1896. And, as everywhere throughout Hapsburgian lands, equestrian and acrobatic acts held fascination for local audiences.

The current war has given the company renewed life, as children come from small towns and villages to seek moments of joy. Audience feedback is immediate, measured by enthusiastic applause for the various acts. This summer's performances for children whose parents are at the front demonstrated once more how important circuses are to Ukrainian life. These performances reminded circus artists in Lviv and elsewhere that the reason for their existence has not faded away. Now, more than ever, Ukraine's children need the kind of unexpected delight that a circus ring has always provided.

37: "And I'll Sing till My Heart Makes a Sound..."

January 10, 2025

Ukraine—indeed, the entire world—of 30 years ago has become almost unrecognizable. Politicians have come and gone, civil uprisings have tossed governments aside, and, unfortunately, Ukraine has suffered untold injury at the hands of a rapacious neighbor.

The rock group Okean Elzy (Eliza's Ocean) has remained among the few constants of everyday Ukrainian life, establishing itself as the country's most famous and successful band. Among its many achievements, albums, and shows, the group's 2018 sold-out Independence Day performance at Kyiv's national sports stadium attracted some 100,000 fans, making it the largest concert in Ukrainian history. Okean Elzy's constant touring inside Ukraine—and around the world—helped establish Ukrainian rock as worthy of international attention.

The group marked its 30th anniversary with an international tour to raise funds for Ukraine. Beginning in September, the group's Lighthouse Tour, promoting its latest English-language album, moved around Europe (Switzerland, France, the Netherlands, Spain, Portugal, and Germany) and North America (Toronto, Montreal, New York, Boston, Philadelphia, Washington, and Cleveland). Each stop added tens of thousands of dollars to the Ukrainian war effort.

The tour's zenith came with three sold-out performances at Kyiv's Palace of Sports, which generated controversy when recruiting officers sought to detain draft-eligible men through document checks as fans left the concert. Meanwhile, the 30th anniversary concert was moved to a bomb shelter underground, with fans singing along as air raid sirens sounded.

The group, led by Svyatoslav Vakarchuk, formed in Lviv from within an earlier band, Klan Tyshi (Clan of Silence). Its first concert under its present name took place in front of the Lviv Opera House in January 1995. It quickly won kudos at various music festivals, making its first appearance in Kyiv in 1996, fronting for Deep Purple. A dozen albums and two dozen singles later—together with soundtracks for animated films and appearances in support of various international causes—and Okean Elzy has become one of Ukraine's most successful international brands.

Okean Elzy's longevity rests in part on the group's stability. In addition to Vakarchuk, drummer Denys Hlinin has been with the band since its foundation in 1994. Bassist Denys Dudko and pianist Miloš Jelić signed on in 2004, while guitarist Vladimir Opsenica came on board a decade later. Former group members Yuri Khustochka, Dmytro Shurov, Pavlo Hudimov, and Petro Chernyavsky have enjoyed success following their departures.

Nearing his 50th birthday, Vakarchuk is perhaps the elder of the Ukrainian rock scene. The son of a pair of university physics professors, he earned a PhD in theoretical physics, launching Okean Elzy while still an undergraduate. He moved to Kyiv and earned notoriety by winning the first grand prize in the Ukrainian version of *Who Wants to Be a Millionaire?* Supporting both the Orange Revolution in 2004–2005 and the Euromaidan revolt of 2013–2014, Vakarchuk was pulled towards politics and served in the Ukrainian parliament. He also spent time as a scholar in residence at Yale and Stanford universities. He joined the Lviv region's territorial defense battalion following the full-scale Russian invasion of 2022. Yet, throughout these activities, music and his band always held pride of place.

The traumas and losses felt by Ukrainians have dominated the band's music during the war. Audiences were particularly moved by two 2022 singles written about the war: "Keimy minnikh zon" ("Flowers of Minefields") and "Misto Marii" ("City of Mary"), in honor of the defenders of Mariupol.

The group's 2024 single, "Voices Are Rising," anchored its concerts across Europe, Ukraine, and North America this autumn. The song speaks powerfully for compatriots living through brutally horrid recent months of war:

Voices are rising
Just let it out right now
Tears that you're hiding
Just let 'em all fall down
And I'll sing till my heart makes a sound
And I'll sing till my heart's breaking out

38: Words and Music of Good Cheer Fill the Air

January 17, 2025

Kyiv's winter holiday celebrations have shifted in recent years, to the Western Julian calendar of December 25 for Christmas and January 1 for New Year's. This leaves behind the Russian Orthodox Church's marking of Christmas on January 7 and Old New Year on January 14, in accordance with the Gregorian calendar.

With these new dates, new traditions have taken shape.

Offerings at Kyiv's October Palace included, for the second year in a row, a "Sinatra Christmas" concert, which is becoming a staple of holiday celebrations for Ukrainians around the country, along with the National Presidential Orchestra's "Magic Christmas Concert" featuring Ukrainian and European holiday music and Strauss waltzes to usher in the new year. The "Diesel Show Big Christmas Concert" followed, headlined by a variety of television actors ranging from pop music stars to comedians, with acts for children to enjoy.

The war was never far from mind. Advertisements for these shows promised that "in the event of an air raid, everyone will wait for blowback in a safe shelter. Then the concert will continue." Ticket proceeds supported various wartime charities.

The shows at the October Palace, overlooking Independence Square, represented only a portion of the festivities during this third wartime holiday season. The national Christmas tree towered over the square before the 11th-century St. Sophia Cathedral, while holiday fairs of various sizes were set up on Podil's Kontraktovyi Square and elsewhere. The city's circus and puppet theater filled with children and their parents, including those who had been wounded at the front. Music clubs and dance halls continued the merriment into early morning.

As in Kyiv, Christmas marts sprang up for holiday celebrations in cities and towns across Ukraine. Skating rinks served as their focal points, with laughter, frost, and a Christmas tree—making ice skating an integral part of the celebration.

Each of these traditions, which have grown stronger during the past three wartime years, marks a turn to celebrating the holidays in ways similar to what takes place in Europe. The holidays have become one more way in which Ukrainians are turning West to confirm their cultural identities.

Ukrainians embrace their own distinctive Christmas customs too. In Lviv, the skating rink, holiday market, and towering Christmas tree on Rynok (Market) Square were joined by the installation of a giant didukh, a Christmas decoration made of wheat and decorated with ribbons. Children in traditional dress sing Ukrainian carols to celebrate yuletide. The Star-Bearers Parade made its way from Muzeyna Square to Rynok Square, with people in costumes carrying bright decorations to the sounds of carols.

The holidays are also a time for reflection. The current war has taken a deep toll on every Ukrainian family. The traumas of violence, destruction, and death require more time to heal than any single Christmas and New Year's celebration. In the meantime, the faithful find solace in their religious rites and beliefs; most Ukrainians delight in the moments they can share with family and loved ones.

Mykola Leontovych's famous New Year's song "Shchedryk" ("The Little Swallow")—known as the "Carol of the Bells" in English—recasts a traditional folk chant. According to the traditional verse, a little swallow flies into the household to proclaim a plentiful and bountiful year ahead. The American lyrics by Peter Wilhousky record the repeating refrain, "One seems to hear, words of good cheer / From everywhere, filling the air." Kyivans and their compatriots throughout Ukraine spent the holiday season searching for words of good cheer and the prosperity that accompanies peace.

39: "Filling the Empty Spaces of My Consciousness"

January 24, 2025

Ukrainian artist Oleksij Dynnyk observed, "For me, painting is primarily art therapy, it motivates to create regardless of whether there is an audience or not, it is also a source of energy recovery, if the process does not bring suffering. So, at the question why I am doing this my answer is very simple: Because it filled all the empty (free) clusters of my consciousness."

Dynnyk wrote these words to introduce three of his remarkable wartime works in the first number of Enzo Comin's zine, which appeared in September. Dynnyk was one of a half dozen Ukrainian artists—the others included Sergei Dobrynov, Zhalobniuk, Mikhail Ray, Maria Drozdova, Alla Volobyeva, Oetri Hrytsiuk—who responded to Comin's open call for submissions to a new, self-published zine, *The Journey*.

Established Italian graphic artist and writer Comin created *The Journey* to fill a gap that existing art magazines do not address by inviting artists to submit works that revolve around what happens in the lives of artists as they create. Dobrynov was among the first to respond, followed by other Ukrainian artists. Comin decided to dedicate the first issue to the remarkable artists working in wartime Ukraine. The result is a haunting, affecting, compelling online collection of 18 works.

Fanzines are nonprofessional and nonofficial publications created by enthusiasts—fans—of a particular cultural phenomenon or moment. The term arose with the first science fiction fanzines dating from the 1940s. Fan-based, self-published magazines took off among sci-fi, sports, and film aficionados, becoming particularly popular with the appearance of the *Star Trek* fan publication *Spockanalia*.

Creators no longer peck away at typewriters to produce mimeographed content that is dropped into mailboxes at their own expense. Twenty-first century technologies and social media platforms have turned them into a popular way for devotees to reach audiences measuring in the tens of thousands worldwide.

Comin established *The Journey* as a virtual vessel for artists to share their ongoing experiences. He initially expected his fellow artists to write about unsuccessful pieces, unexpected changes, and compelling incidents connected to their work. Dobrynov's response immediately elevated the project beyond this intended focus. Comin found Dobrynov's work, as well as that of his compatriots, to demonstrate how Ukrainians want "to convey joy, warmth and kindness of native places" that can no longer be reached because of the war.

The artists' accompanying narratives speak to the poignancy of displacement, the horrors of war, the need to paint by candlelight, and the return to analog techniques as blackouts prevent reliance on electronic technologies. They tell of the traumatizing experiences of living through war.

Maria Drozdova, for example, wrote about living in Kharkiv in February 2022. "The Russian army was constantly shelling the city; there were days when the city was shelled by Russian aircraft and when there was a breach of the city's defense and there were street battles. Then there was a counteroffensive and Kharkiv survived, although shelling from Russia happens now, as well as throughout Ukraine," she wrote.

Alla Volobyaeva's personal horror ran deep, as is reflected in her art. "When the full-scale war began in Ukraine, I was pregnant and had to give birth. I was hiding in the basement of my house, because the Russian bastards were already approaching our house. It's a long story, I'm living in it now," she wrote. Hers is a story which she turned into art.

Such stories and art works spoke powerfully to Comin. As he explains,

> I am influenced by the geographical and social environment of my home region in the northeast of Italy, next to Slovenia. It is the border with the Balkan region and, when I was younger, with Yugoslavia. Currently, I live in a city that was divided into two sectors at the end of the Second World

War, Gorizia, with the eastern side that is Nova Gorica (New Gorizia), Slovenia. Besides that, my region has always been in the center of Europe, in the middle of the entire Mediterranean area, in other words it has involved and brought together all the cultures and peoples that have struggled, evolved and passed from all directions. All my thinking and feeling as an artist, writer and creator of art projects are connected to this fluent and multi-level heritage.

Comin's plans include presentations in Italy and advancing a new novel in Italian—*Harmony of Resistance*—which came out in September. He will shortly open the call for applications to appear in *The Journey's* second issue. As with the last time around, there will be no geographic limits on submissions. Meanwhile, the Ukrainian artists who seized on the opportunity Comin offered the first time will be recording their experiences through art worthy of international attention.

40: "As the Length of the War Began to Be Measured in Weeks"

January 31, 2025

Confronted by the increasing threat of a full-scale Russian invasion in 2022, Vinnytsia midwife, spiritualist, and writer Oleksandra "Sasha" Basko began to record a real-time autobiography. Her powerful war diary tracked her reactions and those of her husband Slava to the outbreak of a war that would forever disrupt their lives. The result is a vivid, raw, and very personal account of wartime, set down as it happened.

A copy of Basko's war diary made its way to New York and, through mutual friends, into the hands of New Orleans-based theater director Natasha Ramer. Ramer immediately envisioned Basko's words as a play. She set out to adapt the diary into a theatrical script that she filmed as *A Non-Fictional War.*

Ramer spent her earliest years in Ukraine and then later years in Lithuania. She graduated from Moscow's Russian Institute of Theatre Arts (GITIS) before becoming one of Lithuania's leading theater directors. She came to the United States in 1982 and, eventually, made her way to New Orleans, where she established Moscow Nights, a cultural education nonprofit. Committed to bringing the arts of East-Central Europe to Louisiana, Moscow Nights has developed a rich program of theatrical and musical events over the past 25 years. For example, a virtual live online performance of Andrei Kureichik's *Insulted. Belarus(sia)* during the COVID shutdown of 2020 gave attention to the vibrant underground theatrical scene in Belarus at that time.

Ramer worked with New Orleans professional actors Erin Cessna and Casey Groves to translate the emotional core of Basko's *A Non-Fictional War* to the stage and screen. The couple's intimate dialogue begins in the days leading up to Russia's full-scale invasion. Sasha is angry, proclaiming that she doesn't "want troops from another country to save us from ourselves." Slava, trying to calm their domestic distress, tells her that he does not "believe Russia will start a war." Once the war begins, Sasha's anger grows as she cries, "they took my world away." Slava, previously unsure that there would be a war, now asks, "what if we suddenly lose the war?" Cessna and Groves add panic to the pathos of Basko's diary.

Vinnytsia, in southwestern Ukraine, had been initially spared much of the damage inflicted on central and eastern Ukraine, having been hit by Russian rockets and drones only sporadically. Then the Russians stepped up their rocket and drone attacks against the city, aiming to destroy Vinnytsia's utilities infrastructure and raise the levels of terror in the city's population. Basko's diary reveals how the city has been traumatized by war. That trauma only heightened as the conflict bears down on the hopes and fears of Ukrainians throughout the country.

In recognizing *A Non-Fictional War* as one of the best films at this year's Barcelona Exceptional Film Festival and The Best Film Festival, the jurors said, "Theatre and cinema should never be at odds. They complement each other perfectly and Natasha demonstrates this in the wonderful feature film where the performance transcends both arts and fuses them into one, full of beauty and drama."

Ramer said that "we could never have achieved the level of success we did without the creativity of our cinematographer and post-production editor, Antony Sandoval, who teaches at Tulane University. Together, we meticulously crafted every scene to bring forth not just the film itself but also a vibrant spectrum of sound, color, and the unique special effects characteristic of experimental cinema."

Basko's written words transcend Ramer's and Sandoval's artistic achievement, stunning as that may be. As soon as she held Basko's diary in her hands, Ramer realized that the young writer had captured the stark horror of war and the turmoil it inflicts on families. Basko's brutal observations express the turbulence that war brings to everyday life. The result is a transformative journey from the depths of despair to resilience. Her diary is a stunning testament to the endurance of the human spirit, a narrative that transcends time and place. Basko converts her personal story into a universal plea to end the agony of all wars.

Ramer underscores Basko's achievement. "While working on the play script," she observes,

> "I was amazed by Sasha's profound metaphysical New Age spiritualism; it opened my awareness to a whole new Ukraine. Throughout the film, during times of stress and need, she deeply connects with the 'angelic' soloist featured in a movement of Mieczław Weinberg's 'Kaddish' Symphony No. 21 performed by the Odesa Philharmonic Orchestra under the direction of Hobart Earle. Through the music, I revealed this deep spiritualism as Sasha ascends to a higher state of being while seeking answers."

Basko, in an intimate exchange with her husband, compellingly speaks for millions when she writes, "As the length of the war began to be measured in weeks, I became more and more resolved in my desire to stay here on our land." As Ramer understood, the arts can capture profound longing more revealingly than any news story.

41: Bringing the Sounds of Ukraine to European Audiences

February 7, 2025

Audiences at this summer's Copenhagen Summer Festival were treated to a masterful performance of Stanislav Lyudkevich's Violin Sonata in A Minor by violinist Natalia Gordeyeva and pianist Violina Petrychenko. Lyudkevich pulls his main theme through different keys and tempos across three movements in this beautiful 1966 composition. He draws on folk themes throughout, providing ample opportunity for the performers to display their virtuosity. Like much of the Ukrainian classical canon, this sonata deserves more widespread attention from performers and audiences than it has received to date. This summer's Danish audience expressed its enchantment with enthusiastic applause.

Lydkevych was born in Habsburgian Poland in 1879 and studied Ukrainian philology at Lviv University. Simultaneously, he explored musical theory with his pianist mother as well as Oleksandr von Zemlinsky in Vienna and Mieczysław Sołtys in Lviv. He taught Ukrainian and Latin languages before helping create a university-level conservatory in Lviv. He would remain at that school for the rest of his career, even as the city transferred from Austrian and Polish rule to German occupation and then Soviet control.

He gained as much fame for his editing of general reference works in Ukrainian as for his music, but he is perhaps best known for his large-scale symphonic works, including *Caucasus*, based on the poem of the same name by Ukrainian bard Taras Shevchenko. This work earned him a state prize in 1964. He was named People's Artist of the USSR in 1969. His Soviet-era success occurred despite his having refused to condemn fellow composer Vasyl Barvinskyi in 1948 following that composer's arrest and sentencing to the Gulag. Lydkevych died at 100, in 1979.

This summer's performance is one among many bringing attention to Ukrainian classical music. The Copenhagen festival, which began in 1969, is noteworthy for promoting chamber music and upcoming talent. Attracting many high-profile musicians, this performance offered an opportunity for Lydkevych's work to gain recognition among a wider classical community.

Violinist Gordeyeva and pianist Petrychenko belong to a generation of dazzling Ukrainian classical performers who have emerged since independence. Gordeyeva began performing in her native Kyiv during the 1990s at the age of seven. She appeared before concert audiences in Ukraine and across Europe as a rising protégé. Gordeyeva returned to Kyiv in 2014 to establish a private music school and enjoyed success promoting Ukrainian classical music at home and abroad. She moved to Denmark, where she is a top-level performer, following the 2022 Russian invasion of Ukraine.

Petrychenko grew up in a musical family in Zaporizhzhia, winning the prestigious Prokofiev International Piano competition during the 1990s, at the age of 12. Her successes took her to Kyiv for more specialized training, and on to further studies in Germany. She has drawn on her success as a composer and performer to promote Ukrainian music. Her 2015 solo album, *Ukrainian Moods*, garnered widespread praise. She is best known for promoting Barvinsky's piano works, which were largely unknown in Europe. In 2023, she established the annual Sounds of Ukraine music festival in Germany to showcase Ukrainian music.

Gordeyeva and Petrychenko represent a generation of increasingly established classical musicians who appear in concert halls across Europe, North America, and Asia. Musicians and audiences recognize their talent and seek out their performances. In turn, these artists are drawing on their recognition to promote the classical repertoire that emerged from Ukraine across a century of turmoil. In doing so, they expand recognition for Ukraine's artistry and enrich the global classical repertoire with works too long ignored.

42: Turning Bombshells into Fireworks, Bullets into Raindrops

February 21, 2025

Throughout the autumn, the well-known Ukrainian band The Hardkiss, led by front woman Julia Sanina, toured North America and Europe. Like other Ukrainian rock musicians, they have been earning money for themselves and for the Ukrainian war effort, spreading the word that international rock fans need to pay attention to the Ukrainian scene. Their appearances at top venues such as New York's Melrose Ballroom in Queens and Los Angeles's Whisky a Go Go place them among music's elite groups.

Fame and fortune are hardly new to Sanina and her bandmates. Now in her 30s, she grew up in a musical family in Kyiv, initially performing on stage when she was three. At 15, she completed studies at Kyiv's Music School of Jazz and Variety Art and earned a graduate degree in folklore at Taras Shevchenko National University of Kyiv a few years later.

Sanina started performing as a vocalist for children's groups and big bands before developing her own style as a vocalist in the group Sister Siren. In late 2011, she teamed up with her future husband, producer Valeriy Bebko, as the pop duo Val & Sanina, performing in Russian and gaining notice in Russia and in Ukraine for their experimental music videos. Soon, they changed their band's name to The Hardkiss and turned to a harder-edged format while performing in English.

Success with their first music video, "Babylon," earned a contract with Sony BMG and, eventually, opportunities to open concerts for visiting American and British rock groups performing in Kyiv. Awards and sales piled up and, in 2016, they were the runner-up in the Ukrainian national selection for the Eurovision Song Contest.

Throughout these years, The Hardkiss established itself as a leading Ukrainian alternative rock and metal group, with tough songs about personal love and loss. Sanina's performance persona seems a long way from her early days with children's groups and big bands. Her lyrics, often written in collaboration with her husband, emerge from a more softhearted space, one perhaps closer to her roots in jazzy ballads.

As Iryna Kalenska wrote a year ago in the German international music magazine *Reflections of Darkness*, "The Hardkiss is a mixture of seemingly incompatible heavy arrangements, melodic parts, deep lyrics and Yulia Sanina's soulful vocals." This combination of tough and tender, visceral and poignant spoke to her generation growing up in a Ukraine that, at times, disappointed more than it achieved.

Well-known Ukrainian rock groups such as The Hardkiss have promoted themselves and their country on extended tours since the full-scale Russian invasion in February 2022. Together, they have established Ukrainian rock as a genre worthy of fan attention through their North American and European visits. A war launched by aggressors intending to bury Ukrainian cultural identity has had the opposite effect. Leading venues that once overlooked Ukrainian rock achievement now book the groups, to enthusiastic audiences.

The war has prompted artists like Sanina to expand their music beyond their previous focus on love, loss, and the difficulties of growing into adulthood. They now give voice to their generation's wartime trauma. In the 2023 music video for "Festival," Sanina combined lyrics about untrustworthy love with thoughts of war. Filmed in wartime Kyiv, the singer wanders the city's bleak streets, proclaiming, "Oh my God. / Hear me tonight / Turn these bombshells into fireworks / Bullets into raindrops / Our pain into my songs / I wanna feel this world as festival."

The video closes with Sanina standing under a spectacular fireworks display. While they wait for such a moment to arrive in life as well as song, The Hardkiss and other leading Ukrainian rock bands are performing to ensure that the world will not forget them.

43: A Stunning Prayer for Ukraine

February 28, 2025

Lviv's Vivere String Quartet released an astonishingly beautiful album October 4, *Prayer for Ukraine*. Recorded at Stanford University and issued by San Francisco-based Phenotypic Recordings, the album's internationally admired ensemble brings together contemporary and Ukrainian classical music expressing the country's wartime travails. In sharing Ukrainian classical music and culture with wider audiences, the musicians hope to provide solace to all who seek it. Proceeds from the album will be donated to nonprofit organizations providing relief in Ukraine.

The track list includes Zoltan Almashi's haunting "Maria's City (Mariupol)," composed in a bomb shelter during that city's three-month siege. Hannah Havrylets's lyrical "To Mary" and "Expressions" represent a Lviv composer gone too soon: Havrylets died on the invasion's third day due because of the lack of appropriate medical care. Almashi's "Carpathian Song," together with Vasyl Barvinsky's solemn "Prayer," adds Ukrainian folk themes to the mix. Authorities destroyed the music of the Lviv-based Barvinsky following his arrest in 1948. He reconstructed these scores and other lost works following his release from the Gulag a decade later.

Each of the group's selections connects expressively to Ukraine's present and past traumas. The players transform the emotional difficulties they experienced in performing the music to create a recording of exceptional passion and beauty.

Violinists Anna Bura and Dmytro Lysko, violist Uslym Zhuk, and cellist Dmytro Nikolayev formed the quartet in 2010 while students at the Lviv National Academy of Music. As the name of the group—Vivere, meaning "to live"—suggests, its members believe that music is integral to Ukrainian life. Music carries the message of independence and freedom for Ukrainians even during the darkest days of occupation and repression.

The quartet has won praise over the past decade and a half for the heart-wrenching poignancy and explosive power of its playing as it has toured throughout Ukraine, Europe, and North America. Its previous programs and recordings of Ivan Karabyt's String Quartet and Johannes Brahams's Quintet combine Ukrainian works with those of the European classical repertoire. This blend remains a signature feature of the group.

Each musician has enjoyed success as a soloist as well as a member of orchestras and large ensembles. Lysko has won additional notoriety for performing on a violin crafted by his carpenter great-great-grandfather. The instrument has been passed down in his family through four generations. His grandfather taught violin in the family's living room, surrounded by violins of all types. Lysko began studying violin at the age of seven.

Each musician hid their instruments when the war started. While far from the front lines, Lviv nonetheless remains within about five minutes flying time for the fastest Russian rockets. Consequently, the quartet practiced while constantly listening for air raid sirens.

Recording *Prayer for Ukraine* proved to be its own harrowing adventure. The quartet members traveled to Warsaw twice on stressful 10-hour bus journeys, first to secure US visas and then to connect to flights to California. Once in the Bay Area, they maximized their recording time by remaining at the studio day and night. Their playing provided hope, joy, and solidarity to one another and to the Ukrainian cause. Those emotions pour out through each track on the album.

In an August 2023 interview with *The New York Times*, violinist Anna Bura underscored the important of music, especially Ukrainian music, at this moment. "Russia says there's no Ukrainian culture, or music, or language," she said. "They want to erase Ukrainian culture. We want to show people we are here." *Prayer for Ukraine* tells the world not only that Ukrainians remain present, but it offers the rest of us unchallenged beauty, elegance, joy, and grace.

44: Creating Rules of the Game for Contemporary Ukrainian Theater

March 7, 2025

When Dmytro Ternovyi and his wife Olga Ternova set out to establish their own theater in 2007, they landed at a school at the edge of a forest. Nothing but trees stood between the school, their theater, and Russia, 14 miles away. The Theatre na Zhukah (Theater on the Beetles) seemed aptly named, given the woodland outside its door. The pair joked that their little theater was the easternmost theater in Europe. The next theater to the east was already someplace else.

Ternova has brought several works to the stage, while Ternovyi has won numerous national and international awards for his writing. He earned special notice for his libretto for the rock opera *Taras Bulba*. Word of their theater spread, and audiences found their way there from central Kharkiv and further afield.

The school has been destroyed by Russian bombs, but the theater, though damaged, has survived and is waiting to be brought back to life.

Ternovyi has come gradually to accept war, along with the strong belief that life must continue. The paradox for Ternovyi and other Kharkiv artists has been that even when the city was semi-encircled in the first year of the war, and when there were almost no people left, culture turned out to be very important for those who remained.

Denied his own stage, Ternovyi has turned to supporting and promoting works written for the Ukrainian stage since the 2022 Russian full-scale invasion. His efforts—together with those of scores of others—is reconceiving how Ukrainian theatrical life will be structured once peace arrives.

In December 2023, Ternovyi joined other theater leaders to launch the Showcase of Ukrainian Drama held at the Playwrights' Theater in Kyiv's Podil district. This gathering presented readings of several plays that had won various dramaturgical competitions across Ukraine in 2023. Those works, in turn, were published in an anthology that, hopefully, will become the first in a series of almanacs celebrating the year's best Ukrainian plays. Directors and publishers have been working to create the Ukrainian Drama Network to promote Ukrainian theater at home and abroad. At least two of the works have been staged in full. These and other plays may be found in 13 languages on the Ukrainian Drama Translations web portal.

Ternovyi and his colleagues are looking to change how Ukrainians and others see contemporary drama. He has written that those Ukrainian theaters paid little attention to his plays, despite a decade of winning various competitions at home and abroad. The writing, staging, publishing, and competition cycles supporting new works have remained separate and distinct. The goal now is to connect playwrights and their works to theater companies so that they can come to life on stage. To do so, various processes must support one another. The December showcase promoted the necessary connections by bringing together a professional audience from across Ukraine's regions, with the support of the Goethe Institute, for a moment of shared free expression and networking.

In addition to seeking out contemporary works for productions in Ukraine, these efforts include competitions for theatrical translation. This kind of contest has yielded the first English publication of Ivan Franko's *Stolen Happiness*, and the first German translation of Lesia Ukrainka's *The Blue Rose*.

Ternovyi and his collaborators are working to ensure that these proceedings become annual events. Their hope is to change the rules of the game for Ukrainian theater in a way that nurtures an environment that is valued as professional, understandable, transparent, and reasonable for everyone. With luck and perseverance, the unending traumas of war can lead to new opportunities on the stage by nurturing a cooperative spirit throughout the theater community

45: Music as the Rocket Fuel of Diversity in Odesa

March 14, 2025

Volodymyr Gitlin fell in love with music as a boy in Kryvyi Rih, 280 miles southeast of Kyiv. He picked up the clarinet by the time he was eight and began studying at a local music school. When the time came, he set off to the Odesa Conservatory for professional training. There, he fell in with other music students who were more interested in the raucous sounds of Odesa's streets and courtyards than in the elevated music found in recital halls.

Gitlin began performing on the street himself, playing his clarinet in pickup contests that demanded bravado, as one musician tried to upstage another. These musical street matches paralleled what happened in New Orleans, which only seemed natural to Gitlin as he worked to perfect his instrument's Dixieland heritage.

Other influences propelled Gitlin's musicianship forward, especially Jewish klezmer music and a local chanson movement that—like the New Orleans battles—encouraged confrontations, with musical instruments as weapons. He and his conservatory pals spread out across Odesa, spurring flash mobs at the Privoz Market, on local streetcars, and along the famous Primorsky Boulevard.

Before too long, a makeshift band took shape, performing at restaurants with a combination of "Odesa gangsta folk" music, as its members called it, and tall tales, anecdotes about old Odesan life, and table-dancing competitions. By 2014, the band had grown from three members (vocals, accordion/double bass, guitar) to seven (original instruments plus clarinet, trumpet, trombone, and drums). The band's reputation went national—and international—when it opened the Odesa Jazz Fest that year under the name Dengi Vpered (Pay Up Front).

Vocalist Bagrat Tsurkan signed on in 2020 as other musicians rotated through. A new music video, "Babushka Zdorova" ("Grandma is Healthy"), had thousands of views on Facebook. Leaving for an international tour in 2021, the group changed its name to Kommuna Lux, to reflect a growing community of like-minded musicians and fans.

The 2022 Russian full-scale invasion of Ukraine changed everything. Some band members went to war. Those who stayed transformed the group into a promotion company to raise money for Ukrainian charities. Emerging at this time as a favored klezmer band in Poland and Germany, the group raised thousands of dollars on its tours for those in need back home. The musicians' rambunctious and rebellious brand of Ukrainian, Jewish, and Eastern European folk music expressed their notion that music brings light, freedom, and many good feelings to their audiences.

The band has continued to play across North America and Europe over the past year, before large and small audiences. No venue is too large—it played in January at New York's Lincoln Center—or too modest, as it performed in community centers, church and synagogue halls, and clubs of displaced Odesans living elsewhere. Every concert includes a blend of music and storytelling, jokes, and tricks, a reminder of Odesa itself. To ensure that the point is not lost, the band prints a newspaper each year full of Odesa lore that it hands out at performances.

Since its founding, Odesa has been a music machine. Attracting residents from across the Russian Empire and the Mediterranean region, all sorts of sounds from all sorts of cultures crashed together, often accompanied by ecstatic dancing. As a young Gitlin understood, music was to be learned in the streets, courtyards, and taverns as well as at the city's renowned conservatory, symphony hall, and opera house. In Odesa, music is the rocket fuel of diversity.

46: Mustached Bards: Revisiting Soviet Ukrainian Pop Music

March 21, 2025

Volodymyr Ivasiuk became a Soviet pop idol and a Ukrainian hero at the age of 19, when his "Chervona Ruta" was performed on a televised song fest in Moscow by the group Smerivhka and became USSR Song of the Year in 1971. Soviet rock legends Sofia Rotaru and Vasyl Zinkevych performed that song and other tunes for the soundtrack for the film *Chervona Ruta,* featuring the young composer's music. It has been covered by numerous singers ever since, including Ukrainian pop heroine Ruslana.

Ivasiuk did not have much time to enjoy his celebrity. The authorities looked at him with increasing skepticism as they realized "Chervona Ruta," or "Red Flower" in English, about a mythical flower which brings love to a young girl, appealed to Ukrainian nationalists as a coded message proclaiming cultural distinctiveness. By the 21st century, the song had become incorporated into the canon of Ukrainian folk music.

Ivasiuk was raised in Chernivtsi before heading off to Lviv to study medicine and musical composition. He managed to balance the two careers throughout his 20s. His "I Am Your Wing," "Ballad about Mallow," and "Ballad about Two Violins" became underground sensations among young Ukrainian nationalists, despite his denial of any political intent. In April 1979, at the age of 30, he received a mysterious phone call. Three days later he was found hanging from a tree in a nearby forest. Police investigators declared his death a suicide. Few believed the official story, though, and an official forensic examination in 2019 concluded that he could not have hanged himself. More than 10,000 people attended his funeral and his legend has grown over subsequent decades.

Ivasiuk's rise was part of an effort by Soviet authorities to counter the tidal wave of music crashing in from the West. Moscow officials instructed local party committees to sponsor bands which exuded approved Soviet values and comportment. Dozens of bands emerged, singing innocent songs which drew on local folk traditions (such as Carpathian folk rhythms) and African American funk music to produce a sound that encouraged young people to dance without passing along shady values. The result was a Soviet pop sound that made the American band The Monkees sound profound.

A few performers such as Ivasiuk created more meaningful music, connecting with as-yet subterranean nationalist sentiments, though scores of Soviet youths abandoned the sound as soon as the country opened up to Western bands in the late 1980s. No one seemed to look back as the Soviet Union disintegrated and its components entered a global music culture. But the tale does not end here, as Shukai Record's Dmytro Prutkin recently explained to Malcolm Jack, pop and rock music editor for Britian's weekly *The Big Issue*: "When Western music came to market, all this Soviet music, it was like, 'it's not interesting. Let's forget about it. It doesn't sound like Pink Floyd. It doesn't sound like Prince. It sounds very common, simple, primitive.'"

A younger generation started searching out records and cassettes at flea markets and found something fresh and intriguing in this sound. The wave of interest grew, prompting filmmakers Vitali Bartdetskyi and Oleksandr Kovsh to pull together a documentary about the sound, *Mustache Funk*, named for the facial hair sported by many of the bands' members. Released in 2021, the film struck a chord with Ukrainian audiences.

Seattle's Light in the Attic Records began working on a compilation of Soviet-era pop music from around the USSR. The Russian full-scale invasion of Ukraine changed these plans, however, leading to the recent issuing of a new collection of Ukrainian language songs dating from 1971 to 1996 that were found in various archives: *Even the Forest Hums*.

This renewed interest in Soviet Ukrainian pop represents more than nostalgia. As listeners—evidently including the KGB—understood when listening to Ivasiuk and others, this music spoke to the desire for an independent Ukraine. Trying to redefine Ukrainian art, music, and literature under existential threat by the full-scale Russian invasion connects Soviet-era culture to those fighting for Ukraine's future today.

47: Talking to the Dead to Heal the Living

March 28, 2025

American actor Joe Spano once observed, "The real hopeful thing about the arts is that you take painful experiences and shape them, you come out of experience like this not devastated, not demolished by it, but hopefully healed or having experienced a catharsis." These words came to John Freedman's mind as he interviewed Spano for the November 4 episode of his *Dictionary of Ukrainian Emotions* podcast. Spano had just finished a dramatic reading of Tetyana Kytsenko's *Call Things by Their Names,* which speaks powerfully to the need to take hold of one's own fate when coming out of painful experiences.

The issue of what we call what is happening around us became acute for Kytsenko at 5 a.m. on the morning of February 24, 2022, when Russian cruise missiles began to rain down around her. Later, she recalled, "We knew what was going on even without news reports. Was this a special operation, a conflict or a crisis? No, not one of these words came to mind, and if these diplomatic definitions are rinsed of their hypocrisy, you will be left with the old standard: War."

Kytsenko explored the meaning of names and identity in the days following the Russian full-scale invasion. Her piece appears in a collection of 20 plays written by Ukrainian dramatists in response to that invasion. Compiled, edited, and introduced by Freedman, *A Dictionary of Emotions in a Time of War: 20 Short Works by Ukrainian Playwrights* captured the experiences of 18 members of Kyiv's Theater of Playwrights.

The book won awards and sold well. Several of the plays have had successful readings at theaters around the world; some have had full-fledged productions. Freedman wanted to expand their reach, and, at the encouragement of Kharkiv playwright Dmytro Ternovyi, who has been a prime mover in the project, entered into partnership with the Ukrainska Pravda website to create a series of nine podcasts posted over late 2024 into 2025.

The podcasts present works by nine contributors to the original volume: Kytsenko, Anastasia Kosodii, Oksana Grytsenko, Oksana Savchenko, Andrii Bondarenko, Irina Garets, Olga Matsiupa, Liudmila Timoshchenko, and Maksim Kurochkin. Each play is read by an American or British actor: Alessandra Torresani, Kristin Milward, Joe Spano, Kevin McMongale, Kathleen Chalfant, Jessica Hecht, Sharon Washington, and Kosovar American actor Kushtrim Hoxha. Hoxha's own experiences fleeing the former Yugoslavia to the United States at a time of war added poignancy into the reading of Kurochkin's *Pobut* (*Everyday Life*).

Freedman follows up the readings by interviewing the actors about their reactions to the texts. The result is an amplification of the printed word, when each actor talks about personal experience. This helps lift the Ukrainian works into a universal emotional landscape.

For example, Milward's interpretation of Savchenko's powerful play *I Want to Go Home* speaks to sudden and astonishing dislocations, as the protagonist wrestles with whether to abandon her elderly parents in a destroyed Mariupol. Initially, she creates a conundrum: either they leave together or die together. But is this really the only choice? She decides to leave, and they decide to stay. She leaves and tries to remain in touch, though she feels ashamed. Her thoughts turn to a school friend who remained in Bucha, wondering if she was blown to bits during the brutal atrocities there. Images of her defenseless parents, her 12-year-old daughter who is no longer fearful of air raid sirens, a lover reachable only with spotty internet connections fill her with hatred and anger. Hatred makes it hard to breathe, she says, and makes you want to kill the ones who kill you. The reaction is physiological and can't be explained. The reading by a masterful artist like Milward makes this story into penetrating, universal art.

The first podcast in the series, featuring Torresani reading Kosodii's short post-dramatic monologue "How to Talk to the Dead," was inspired by photos of those who died in Russian atrocities in cities like Bucha, Irpin, Mariupol, and others. The need to speak to the dead became palpable, but how to do so? "No special workshops are required," Kosodii counsels. "We determine our dead to be a fact of life, we tell stories about them, invent stories so that your dead will speak through them.... Suddenly there will be such words as there never have been.... Your people were alive as they wished to be."

In the interview with moderator Freedman, Kosodii observed that there is no time to grieve in a time of war. We need different tools to mourn, she said, and talking to the dead creates a new language to talk about everything. We need to invent stories so our dead will speak through them. We need to do so in an ethical way. Ukrainian writers—and playwrights in particular—are tasked with finding these stories to speak to the living.

48: Capturing the Power of Ukrainian Folk Traditions on Film

Villagers in western Ukraine liven the dark days of December and January with the traditional festival of Malanka, which combines pre-Christian and Christian traditions. Carolers (usually teenage girls) head out at sunset, moving from house to house to stave off the evil spirits that rule the darkness. Each household spreads out a ritual "kutia" banquet of blood sausage called Malanka, sweet breads, and dumplings to offer the carolers. The more abundant the meal, the better the promise of the year ahead.

Young men lead the way, dancing in masks to scare away ill-intended spirits. Young women and their mothers carefully assess the leaping dancers, trying to spot a worthy candidate for marriage. The next morning, the men head to a local crossroads to ignite the didukh, a sheaf of grain, and jump over the resulting bonfire. The men then sow the seeds for the spring crops, marking the end of darkness as the days grow longer.

Each village embraced its own version of the celebration, with some rites travelling with Ukrainian immigrants to the prairies of Canada. Ukraine's brutal 20th century of war, revolution, occupation, pogroms, famine, political suppression, industrialization, and urbanization nearly wiped the tradition out. But every once and a while, a city youth visiting grandparents down on the farm witnessed these bright displays of villager folkways and wanted to bring that experience to the post-Soviet city. Filmmaker Dmytro Sykholytkyy-Sobchuk was one such captivated youth.

Approaching his 30th birthday, Sykholytkyy-Sobchuk was looking for a suitable subject for his first feature-length film. The movie he made, *Pamfir*, tells the story of a former smuggler, as he returns to his native village after years of working abroad. He has come home to set a good example for his teenage son, arriving on the eve of the local Malanka celebrations. A crime cartel controls everything going on in the region, and eventually Pamfir's good intentions meet harsh local realities. Meanwhile, his son, attempting to keep his father from leaving, sets fire to his documents and, in the process, burns down a local house of prayer. Pamfir returns to his life of crime to pay off the bill for the damage his son caused with the fire.

Visually stunning, the film's success capturing Ukrainian folk motifs gained special notice as the Russians launched their full-scale invasion. Made prior to full-scale fighting, it touches on some of the large themes of wartime Ukraine and became a powerful expression of the unbreakable spirit, resistance, and renewal of a country under attack.

Sykholytkyy-Sobchuk's film uses the gorgeous backdrop of the Malanka carnival, with beautifully costumed carolers and dancing devils moving in and out of the forests surrounding the village. The costumes, songs, and dances become a major part of the story, recapturing earlier folk traditions that many Ukrainians feared had disappeared. The film becomes a tale of resilience, one that speaks powerfully to Ukrainians trying to hold on to their culture and values at a time of peril.

The film faced many obstacles along the way, including COVID shutdowns, which brought production to a halt. But in May 2022, it premiered at the 75th Cannes Film Festival, where it won immediate honors. Further praise followed at various international film festivals, with *The Guardian* labelling it one of the best films of 2023. It subsequently entered wide distribution, including release on Netflix.

Pamfir's costumes formed the core of an exhibit at Ukraine House in Copenhagen this winter. *Malanka: The Dance of Death and Life* featured over 30 outfits and 80 masks from the film, together with props, sketches, storyboards, and video. Exhibit curator Oleksii Ananov explained, "The night is the longest at that time, and the border with the other world becomes thin, which is why various demons come to our world to appease, outwit, or defeat us in a competition. This struggle is going on right now, and for the sun to rise in the morning, you have no right to sleep but must join the carnival and defeat the forces of darkness in this frantic dance."

Shortly after Pamir's opening at Cannes, Sykholytkyy-Sobchuk made a short documentary for *The New Yorker* chronicling the stories of Ukrainian sculptors who temporarily left their work creating religious statues in order to build tank traps. Entitled *Liturgy of Anti-Tank Obstacles: When Artists Prepare for War*, the documentary premiered at the Sarajevo Film Festival in August 2022.

Both films touch on the power of Ukraine's traditions and continuing cultural enhancement to offer the strength required to persevere, fending off the darkness for the better days ahead.

49: Grassroots Arts Comfort and Inspire Ukraine's Frontline Troops

Some among Ukraine's frontline commanders have embraced the power of the arts to comfort and inspire their forces since the very beginning of the war. As reported in this blog series in April 2022, internationally acclaimed Kyiv street artist Sasha Korban joined the Ukrainian war effort as soon as the war began. When he reported for duty, his commander immediately sent him out to the capital's streets to paint, even as Russian forces were closing in on the city. Korban's moving street mural depicting two gaunt hands gently sewing together a tattered Ukrainian flag brilliantly caught the precarious moment when patriotism faced off against doubt.

Korban and his commander were not alone in appreciating the power of art to shape what happened along front lines. Around the same time, Odesa television and film star Mykolay Serga enlisted to defend his city and country. His commander, like Korban's, recognized that Serga's talent offered a powerful tool for raising morale and preserving the mental health of fighters engaged in daily battles. As Serga recently told Toronto *Globe and Mail* reporter Vladislav Golovin, "The stress was palpable. We couldn't sleep despite our exhaustion. I decided to gather those who were off duty and read them poetry." His comrades were able to sleep that night for the first time since the fighting began.

Some wounded soldiers have turned their talents to entertaining troops, even as they are no longer able to join them on the front lines. Zaporizhzhya classical singer Yuriy Ivaskevich has been performing as part of his rehabilitation after losing his left leg on the battlefield in 2023. So too did conservatory-trained violinist Olha Rukavishnikova, who lost an eye while serving as a gunner in a counteroffensive around Kharkiv.

More senior commanders took note of what Korban, Serga, and other artists and performers were achieving. Within the war's first weeks, the armed forces established the Cultural Forces group, bringing together musicians, actors, writers, and other artists serving in the army to perform for their fellow soldiers. Each month, Cultural Forces perform nearly 600 concerts for small groups of soldiers on break at the front.

Entertainers performing for soldiers is nothing new. These stories distinguish the current war in Ukraine by systematically drawing on talent among the soldiers themselves rather than from visits by touring performers. The concerts have become integrated into platoon and brigade life, further building a collective identity among those who are fighting every day. Beyond performances, Cultural Forces has delivered 20,000 books to soldiers at the front.

Such initiatives reveal the appreciation of Ukraine's highest-ranking officers for the importance of culture within their overall strategy. These battlefield accomplishments have prompted Cultural Forces to send their artists on international tours—with more than 170 concerts organized in the US alone—to generate support for the Ukrainian war effort.

Performing for fellow soldiers has inspired the artists in return. Serga, for example, equipped a bus as a mobile music studio, which he takes with him to record songs with the troops at the front. So far, nearly two dozen of these efforts have been released via the internet.

General Vladyslav Klochkov of the General Directorate of Moral and Psychological Support, when speaking with journalist Golovin, repeated the lessons learned early on by the commanders of Sasha Korban and Mykolay Serga. "The guitar and the violin also could be a weapon," Klochkov told Golovin, and "The person who graduated from music school could be more useful as a musician in the army than as a soldier with a rifle, sitting at an observation point."

Culture has been central to the war in Ukraine from its earliest days. Beginning with Putin's numerous proclamations that there is no such thing as "Ukrainian culture," this conflict has been about more than territory and material gain. The meaning of Ukrainian culture has stood—and continues to stand—at the very center of why Russia invaded Ukraine, and why Ukrainians have responded so steadfastly.

50: Three Years of Trauma, and of Creativity

February 14, 2025

There is no reason for joy on this, the end of the third year of Russia's full-scale invasion of Ukraine. Far too many people have died; far too many villages, towns, and cities have been destroyed; far too many lives have been ruined; far too much trauma has been inflicted. Yet Ukraine holds and even rises. For a nation proclaimed by its enemy not to exist, Ukrainian identity has never appeared stronger. Ukraine's staunch defense of its nationhood stands at the center of this achievement. Its cultural vigor is not far behind.

As I wrote a year ago, the more Russian forces try to destroy Ukrainian culture, the more it asserts itself. Adaptable Ukrainian artists in every genre have kept creating, no matter what the Russians have thrown at them. The arts rise into prominence whenever danger wanes. The war has revealed an artistic sensibility that draws on tradition to create exciting new cultural forms.

Ukraine's cultural response to this war began before the full-scale invasion of 2022. Ukrainians embraced their shared future in 2014, when Russia seized Crimea and touched off fighting in Donetsk and Luhansk. Many who spoke Russian before switched to speaking Ukrainian as a symbol of a newfound common identity. New generations of creators had reached maturity. Young Ukrainians with no memory of the Soviet Union, secure in their knowledge of the Ukrainian language no matter what they spoke at home, looked westward for inspiration. Putin and far too many other Russians mistook Ukraine's cultural churning as a sign of cultural deficiency. We now know that it was a sign of strength, as a new cultural cement began to bond Ukrainians together.

Cultural development always is asynchronous, moving ahead at different speeds in various dimensions until suddenly something new emerges. This is the story of Ukrainian culture prior to the Russian full-scale invasion. Cinema, the visual arts, literature, popular and classical music, theater, and dance evolved separately until, under the pressure of Russian aggression, they merged into a powerful expression of shared Ukrainian identity. This weaving together of once separate cultural strands runs through the past three years.

Prior achievements—distinctly Ukrainian traditions in the visual arts, too-often-overlooked works in classical musical, long repressed theatrical movements—are embraced once more. So too are art forms not necessarily thought of as distinctly Ukrainian, such as modern dance, rock music, and cinema. Artists in these fields have responded to the unrelenting burdens of war by creating remarkable works which promise to withstand the forces of time.

The war has also brought Ukrainian cultural achievements to the attention of the international community. From dance and orchestral tours to theater festivals and art exhibits, many around the world have been given the chance to discover Ukrainian cultural accomplishments. As the war's third year ends, artists and works once identified as "European" or "Russian" are being correctly reclassified as "Ukrainian." Ukrainian dancers are performing on stages worldwide. Ukrainian plays appear in as diverse locales as London, New York, and Hong Kong. Ukrainian rock groups tour Europe and North America. Ukrainian symphonic music finds its way onto concert programs from Berlin to Buenos Aires and from South Africa to Korea. By denying the existence of Ukrainian culture, the Russian war machine has prompted many to find Ukrainian creativity for the first time.

Viewing war through the lens of culture helps us consider possible outcomes. In military terms, this is a war of attrition; it will end when one of the combatants is no longer able to fight. Culturally, there can be no resolution to this conflict simply by drawing new lines on maps, swapping territory, or exhausting all the resources—human and material—that are available to each side. Unless we bring a cultural dimension to the peace table, any cessation of hostilities will be a pause rather than an end.

Twenty-first century wars in particular have been about more than elites, natural resources, and strategic advantage. They are about cultural identity. Culture does not sit on the sidelines of contemporary conflict. It is central to it.

Concluding Observations

So many in the world of foreign affairs and military expertise miscalculated how the Russian full-scale invasion of Ukraine would play out. Like Vladimir Putin, they could only image Russia rolling over Ukraine in a matter of weeks. Once again, as has happened so many times throughout history, a smaller but spunky nation has held off far more powerful marauders. The experts simply did what experts do. Rather than consider spirit, the will to resist, and other intangibles, they counted what turned out to be under-maintained Russian tanks and under-provisioned Russian soldiers. They might have done better had they counted the number of Ukrainian hip-hop groups.

The world seemed taken aback when President Volodymyr Zelinsky quipped that he didn't need a ride, he needed ammunition. Zelinsky spoke for millions of his compatriots. Ever since independence, Ukrainians—especially those too young to have memories of life in the Soviet Union—defined themselves through an increasingly vibrant cultural scene. The arts mattered.

Like many of my colleagues, I underestimated the Ukrainian will to resist. Having watched postindependence Ukrainian culture develop, I should have known better. Raucous anti-regime demonstrations at ballet performances, unending Ukrainian-language rock performances proclaiming freedom, and ever expanding Ukrainian literary and theater scenes offered signs of a deep-seated will to resist. Having at least a passing knowledge of these developments should have helped me appreciate how the war would be fought.

Before continuing, I need to make clear that none of the cultural developments chronicled here offset the unending traumas brutally imposed by Russia's war on Ukraine. The hardships and horrific losses inflicted by the war will cast a long, tragic shadow over Ukraine for decades to come. The arts can't win a war; they can and will shape the peace, however.

The stories contained in this volume trace Ukrainian artistic expression during the war's third year. Collectively, they tell of resilience and the consolidation of a new Ukrainian culture. Events reviewed from the war's first year revealed a powerful impulse for cultural survival and resistance to the Russian threat. These trends matured during the war's second year, as the arts emerged as a powerful sign of Ukrainian resilience. The essays here speak of strengthening cultural expression. In other words, the arts have moved over the past three years from supporting survival to shouting resistance, from encouraging to securing a new cultural foundation.

Survival

Survival remained top of mind for the Ukrainian arts community, as for all Ukrainians, during the hours, days, and weeks following the 2022 Russian invasion. Cultural figures and institutions immediately set out to do what they could to help their country resist the invading Russians while the demands of war shut down prewar activities.

Theater and dance companies directed their costume departments to sew uniforms, camouflage netting, and first aid supplies. Puppet theaters set up programs to help traumatized children push aside their fears. Cultural institutions in western Ukraine welcomed counterparts fleeing from eastern Ukraine into their creative communities. Classical musicians in Kyiv and Kharkiv performed in metro stations converted into makeshift bomb shelters. Famous rock groups came together on YouTube to perform songs airing anger at the Russians; street artists took their spray cans out to add poignant patriotic murals to cityscapes. Artists in disparate genres discovered that they could play a role in helping Ukraine survive by being themselves.

Unprecedented international collaboration to save Ukrainian artistic achievements took shape in a matter of days. These joint international and Ukrainian partnerships supported a massive effort to move Ukraine's cultural artifacts to safety. These programs have grown over the past three years into one of history's largest cultural rescue missions.

The international theater community came together to launch the Worldwide Ukrainian Play Readings initiative, commissioning playwrights to write new works about the war. These commissions support the authors and, through translation projects, bring dozens of new Ukrainian plays to audiences around the world.

Universities established residences for Ukrainian writers; publishers in the West brought out dozens of new works in translation. Dance companies—such as the Dutch National Ballet Academy—invited Ukrainian dancers to join them during these early days, as did Budapest circus schools. Established Ukrainian rock singers, musicians, dancers, and opera stars toured Europe and North America at various times to raise money for the Ukrainian war effort at home.

These activities took flight with remarkable speed, enabling the arts in Ukraine to survive the opening salvos of war. There was little time to spare. Russian commanders understood that this was a war about culture as well as territory. Their troops savagely attacked and pillaged libraries, museums, art galleries, theaters, and concert halls wherever they went.

Resistance and Resilience

By summer 2022, the existential focus on survival transformed into a culture of resistance as both sides settled in for a long war of attrition. A vibrant club scene returned to Kyiv. The Lviv Organ Hall, taking advantage of its safer location further from the front, booked international touring classical musicians. The Lviv National Ballet staged full-length performances. Theaters and concert halls opened new seasons in accordance with regulations imposed by martial law (including limiting audiences to the size of a venue's bomb shelter).

The 2022 holiday season marked a turning point, as puppet theaters in Kyiv and Lviv mounted special shows and holiday concerts in Kyiv and Odesa attracted enthusiastic audiences. Each new production represented a statement of defiance to the Russian invasion.

Writers and visual artists found ways to express their hostility to the Russians as well. Powerful wartime poems, short stories, novels, and films took shape. Professional and amateur artists converted the detritus of war left behind by the Russians into pieces of art. The reuse of captured Russian war wreckage reached an apogee of sorts in June 2023, when composer Roman Hryhoriv stepped onto the stage of St. Andrew's Church, Kyiv's Baroque jewel box, to perform his new concertino for MRLS BM-27 Uragan missile and chamber orchestra.

Some in the arts highlighted past and present-day achievements in defiance of President Putin's declaration that there is no such thing as Ukrainian culture. Music enthusiasts, for example, created databases for classical and electronic music, offering aficionados one-stop shops to discover Ukrainian musicianship. Rock stars integrated traditional folk music and instruments into their shows. Ukrainian music in all its forms made its way onto Western concert stages, where it never had been before.

Major book, film, and theater festivals returned to Kyiv by the war's second year, and art galleries around the country presented shows focused on Ukrainian themes. In Kharkiv, among the most punished frontline cities, enthusiasts found spaces tucked away in corners protected from direct attack to present art and photography exhibits.

Collectively and individually—as chronicled in my previous two collection of essays—Ukrainians proclaimed that they had a vibrant culture of their own. One that was thriving despite continuing Russian efforts to deny and destroy its accomplishments.

Strengthening

The artistic trends of the war's third year chronicled here mark a further evolution of the Ukrainian cultural scene. If the arts focused on survival at war's beginning and on resistance and resilience in the months beyond, these stories represent a consolidation of those achievements into a strengthened contemporary arts scene.

As the story about teenage playwrights working with New York theaters reveals, a generation of artists coming of age from the beginning of the war is making its presence felt. These newcomers are redefining several genres, ranging from rappers such as Skofka and poets such as Oksana Rubaniak to playwrights Taya Fedorenko and Uliana Klimchuk.

They can do so because new institutional arrangements, like Kyiv's Film.UA studios and Lviv's Jam Factory Art Center, are proving capable of supporting their work. Some already existing groups, such as Kharkiv's Theatre na Zhukah (Theater on the Beetles) and Kyiv's DVRZ Design Days, have broadened their focus to encourage greater cooperation within their artistic communities. As with Kyiv's Theatre of Playwrights, the infrastructure supporting cultural creativity has deepened during the war.

International partners and funders, such as Germany's Goethe Institute and the British Council, are part of the robust support for Ukrainian culture. Of perhaps greater significance is the fact that Ukrainian works are finding new champions. Ukrainian plays appear regularly on London and New York stages and have enjoyed success as far away as Buenos Aires and Hong Kong. Internationally renowned artists, such as Alexei Ratmansky in dance and Ruslana in music, have generated renewed interest in Ukrainian creativity. Ukraine's cultural ecosystem stands ready to support a robust cultural scene once peace arrives.

Ukrainian artists are creating works worthy of continuation. Artistic organizations throughout Ukraine are supporting noteworthy projects. Lviv National Opera ballet company premiered an ambitious new work, *Light from the Shadows,* grounded in Mykhailo Kotsyubnytsky's monumental folklore-based novel, *Shadows of Forgotten Ancestors.* Catherine Penkova's *Legends of Kyiv,* opening at the Theater of Drama and Comedy on the Left Bank, celebrated the capital's long and distinguished history. Radu Poklitar's outstanding Kyiv Modern-Ballet Theater has continued to produce stunning new works throughout the war. Dmytro Moiseev's exquisite feature film *Grey Bees,* based on Andrey Kurlkov's novel, similarly took shape despite the exigencies war. These works—and many more—are certain to remain part of the standard Ukrainian repertoire into the future.

The stories recorded here, from the third year of war, celebrate a creativity which transcends the necessity of survival, the desire to resist, and the ability to regenerate. This has been a year when the arts in Ukraine have demonstrated their capacity to deepen and extend their reach in new directions. It simultaneously has been a year of untold hardship, deep trauma, and shocking destruction throughout Ukraine and Ukrainian society.

If the arts offer a powerful counter-story to the ongoing combat, it is because, as Iulia Bentia and Pavlo Shopin report in their examination of wartime theater, art responds "to the new reality, participates in various ways in relevant public discussions that try to understand the drama of modern war, and creates a safe space for common emotional reliving a new tragic experience." As these essays remind us, we should always include the arts in our thinking about the present; and the future.

Acknowledgements

This project would have been impossible without the enthusiastic support of Mykhailo Minakov and Izabella Tabarovsky, the editors of the Kennan Institute's *Ukraine Focus* blog at the Wilson Center. Master copy editor Sabrina Detlef improved my initial drafts through her rigorous enforcement of proper grammar, style, and logic. The support and efforts of the entire Kennan Institute staff have been indispensable throughout the writing and production of this book, as with the first and second volumes of *The Arts of War* series. I wish to thank Michael Kimmage, William Pomeranz, Jennifer Wistrand, Joseph Dresen, Lenny Lopato, Victoria Pardini, Dan White, and others for making this series possible. A special thanks is due to Scott Buchholtz for preparing the index.

More than most authors, I have been especially indebted to the many artists from across Ukraine, Europe, Asia, and the United States who have been willing to respond to my queries at this most challenging time. Whenever possible, Ukrainian artists have participated directly in the presentation of their own stories. I particularly wish to express my gratitude for cooperation, insights, and criticisms over the past years from Philip Arnoult, Harley Balzer, Marjorie Mandelstam Balzer, Leah Batstone, Volovymyr Boiko, Olena Bondareva, Hanna Bondarewska, Alex Borovenskiy, Patrick Breslin, Angelene Brookshire, Barbara Bryan, Laura Cahill, Irena Chalupa, Dora Chomiak, Donald Chung, Enzo Comin, Vladislav Davidzon, Taras Demko, Olga Diatel, Yulia Dunaeva, Hobart Earle, John Freedman, Aakhu Freeman, Myroislava Ganyushkina, Alexander Gavrilov, Daniel Gerroll, Melinda Harding, Linda Hodsoll, Ulrike Janssen, Alona Karavai, Lesa Khomenko, Sydnee Lipset, Andriy May, Sonya Michel, Natalia Mouissenko, Yevhen Nemchenko, Anton Ovchinnikov, Dassia N. Posner, Yaroslav Pylynsky, Tatyana Rappaport, A. Lorraine Robinson, Ari Roth, Viktor Ruban, Kateryna Smagliy, Diana Taras, Dmytro Ternovyi, Carlos Uriona, Yury Urnov, Walter Ruby, Wing Sze, Diana Taras, William Wong, and Tetiana Zaharchenko.

In the end, these essays are about the indominable spirit and inspiring creativity of the artists about whom I have written. These stories are completely their own. I am honored to do what I can to call attention to them. Together, they reflect the power and grandeur of the Ukrainian people who, when it mattered most, banded together to proclaim their dignity, courage, and reality.

Blair A. Ruble
Washington, DC
March 2025

About the Author

Blair. A. Ruble is a Washington-based writer. He was a Distinguished Fellow at the Wilson Center in Washington, DC prior to April 2025. He previously served as the center's vice president for programs and the director of its Kennan Institute. Educated at the University of North Carolina and the University of Toronto, he is the author of eight book-length works. His 2016 book, *The Muse of Urban Delirium: How the Performing Arts Paradoxically Transform Conflict-Ridden Cities into Centers of Cultural Innovation*, is now available in Ukrainian translation. Collections of his culture essays appeared in 2023 and 2024 as *The Arts of War: Ukrainian Artists Confront Russia, Year One* and *Year Two*. He received an honorary doctorate from the Ukrainian Modern Art Research Institute in 2012.

Index